**INSTRUCTOR'S EDITION**

Beginning Level

# LEARNING TO LISTEN IN ENGLISH

Virginia Nelson

**National Textbook Company**
a division of *NTC Publishing Group* • Lincolnwood, Illinois USA

## About the Author

Virginia Nelson is a lecturer in the Summer Session ESL Program at Cornell University and a curriculum writer for a Title VII science-based whole literacy program in Tempe, Arizona.

Published by National Textbook Company, a division of NTC Publishing Group.
© 1997 by NTC Publishing Group, 4255 West Touhy Avenue,
Lincolnwood (Chicago), Illinois 60646-1975 U.S.A.

# Contents (including a list of discrete subjects covered in each activity)

# Introduction

*Learning to Listen in English* is a complete language acquisition program for beginning students of English and native speakers of English who are working on communication improvement. Newcomers to the English language already have language and culture. Their thirst for interesting learning requires that the materials we use contain content in addition to language skills development. For this reason, *Learning to Listen in English* presents content-area information on a variety of subjects.

English language instructors want one program that will take the beginning student all the way to early intermediate status. Because *Learning to Listen in English* spirals language in the content areas and includes drill, review, and intensive listening experiences, it is suitable for the complete beginning language course.

*Learning to Listen in English* is sequenced to familiarize the user with some of the basic vocabulary and structures of English. Vocabulary and structures grow slightly more complex as the learner progresses through the book. However, the level of critical thinking skills required is not hierarchical from activity to activity throughout a unit. This kind of format reflects the real experiences listeners encounter when they negotiate communication in English—at times simple and straightforward, at times intense and challenging. In this regard, every attempt has been made to maintain a likeness to the real world in *Learning to Listen in English*.

*Learning to Listen in English* moves slowly at the beginning of each topic. Each unit contains a variety of exercises so that even students who find English and/or listening extremely challenging can master the topic. This format also meets the needs of native speakers of English who are working on language processing skills in developmental classrooms. Because all the activities are recorded, students may use *Learning to Listen in English* independently as well as in the language classroom.

*Learning to Listen in English* does not contain written instructions because beginning students often do not understand them. Students use and understand all the print on every page. Ten of the fifteen units contain dialogues that provide models of natural language. In each unit, students practice useful activities such as completing charts and agendas and filling in calendars and schedules.

Instructors will find the Scope and Sequence helpful in writing course objectives and lesson plans. *Learning to Listen in English* integrates all four language skill areas and provides a complete program for instructors and users.

## Vocabulary Selection

Every student of English has a different set of lexical needs. A third grader spends weekends with her astrophysics professor mother, listening to her conversation with colleagues. Two refugees, musicians, decide to research an auditions ad they see on a downtown kiosk. Another newcomer moves from street vendor to storefront cook to chef at a posh restaurant, and suddenly needs to interview and hire kitchen staff. A civil engineer is in the United States to represent her consulting firm on a huge roads project. A high school student wants to join the stamp club, but can't keep up with the banter at their meetings. *Learning to Listen in English* contains activities aimed at common initial needs: understanding numbers and letters, giving information about residences, and completing schedules and agendas. The vocabulary selection gives users the confidence to attempt to speak the language. The activities include simple conversation starters that can facilitate casual exchanges on campus, in the neighborhood, or at the office.

## Structure Selection

Many students of English believe that learning the vocabulary and mastering the structure rules will convert them into proficient speakers. Although research in language acquisition does not support this belief, we must make our students comfortable and confident. *Learning to Listen in English* includes intensive drill in common structures, concentrating on asking and answering questions. The sentences are long enough to reflect natural speech, and embedded clauses are left for subsequent courses.

## Organization of the Units

The units provide students with content area and communicative experiences from the start of the course. Each unit involves users more in making decisions about how to complete the activities. Unit 6 introduces dialogues from which listeners must extract certain data. The activities in *Learning to Listen in English* progress from rote retelling of a cue to analysis of information supplied by a conversation to synthesis of data for filling in charts.

## Components

The program consists of the student workbook, four audiocassettes, and this instructor's edition. In the tapescript section of this book, each page from the student workbook is reproduced, with answers set off in large, bold type. Instructions for completing the activities along with other recorded material, which the students will hear but will not see in their books, is conveniently provided in writing with the reproduced student pages.

A separate answer key for individual student use is also available.

# Strategies for Classroom Use

*Learning to Listen in English* is a complete program for beginning students of English as a second/foreign language or native speakers of English who want to accelerate their language processing capabilities. The program may be used successfully in ESL, EFL, or language arts classrooms or for independent study.

Instructors who are native speakers of English may either read the tapescript or play the cassette in the sections where there is no dialogue. The cassette provides excellent modeling when the instructor is not a native speaker, as well as variety in the classroom where the instructor is a native speaker. Finally, the cassette allows individuals to use the materials without an instructor, whether at a mini-lab in the language classroom, in a formal language laboratory, or at home.

The only procedure an instructor needs to keep in mind is to allow emergent speech to emerge. Aggressive communicators might want to speak after the very first lesson. These students should be encouraged to give three to five examples like those in the activity for other students to practice. Likewise, in a cooperative learning classroom, the student in each group who feels most like talking should practice the modeled exercise with the help of the group. Also keep in mind that students acquiring English should speak when *they* decide to, and never before.

Here is a suggested procedure to follow for Unit 1, Activity A:

- Write a few letters on the board, and say them to the class.

- If students seem to be saying letter names to themselves, give them the opportunity to say the names of three to five letters aloud.

- Play the cassette and listen to the letters *A* through *M*. Use the *pause* button on your tape player to give students about five seconds of processing time – time to digest the listening.

- Write the first two items in Part 1 on the board.

- Play the first item and push the *pause* button.

- Write the answers on the board. Have the students look at the answers in their books.

- Play the second item and push the *pause* button.

- Write the answers on the board. Have the students write them in their books.

- Play the rest of Part 1 and have the students write the answers in their books.

- Repeat the above steps for Part 2 of Activity A.

- While the students are working, walk around to make an informal assessment of the level of difficulty for most of the students.

Depending on your assessment:

1. Repeat the lesson if most students cannot do it. Use the *pause* button frequently to interrupt the recording and give students time to hear the answer and write it.

2. Close the lesson if most students were successful.
   a. The best closure is student generated; have any students who want to speak give one item like those in this activity for classmates to do on the board or at their seats.
   b. At this level of communicating, students may not be willing to speak to the class. Thus, you can close the lesson by writing three letters on the board and listening while one or more students say them.
   c. If none of the students wants to speak, write three letters on the board and ask a student to point to each one as you say its name.
   d. If none of the students wants to work at the board, simply write three letters on the board and say the name of each letter.

The above procedure can be modified for use with any of the activities in the book.

# Extension and Practice Activities

*Learning to Listen in English* may be used in an intensive English program or for a year-long course. In either situation, instructors may wish to use extension and practice activities such as the following to help students integrate the language skills and accelerate their language acquisition or improvement. The activities listed in this section are intended for students to do while the instructor observes and advises. Instructors will have to interpret and model suggestions, and provide students with the opportunity to practice speaking alone or in groups.

### Unit 1: Letters and Numbers

Students can:

- make charts with letters and numbers and drill each other on both
- map twenty U.S. cities that are not mentioned in the text
- buy a newspaper that lists high and low temperatures for U.S. cities and record the cities and temperatures on a chart
- graph temperatures by geographic region
- map twenty world cities that are not mentioned in the text
- alphabetize lists of U.S. and world cities
- spell city names to each other
- make a local map

### Unit 2: Clock Time

Students can:

- compile a personal agenda of daily and weekly activities
- make an agenda for three classmates
- obtain a bus timetable from the local bus station
- map ten bus routes and record the departure/arrival times to and from each location

### Unit 3: Calendar Time

Students can:

- make a calendar for the month in progress
- make a calendar for the year in progress
- make a personal activity calendar
- make an activity calendar for three classmates

### Unit 4: Money

Students can:

- obtain bus, train, and plane fares from travel agents or the newspaper
- list fares from your location to ten other locations
- graph fares by geographic region
- buy tickets from each other using play money and authentic fare schedules

### Unit 5: The Planets

Students can:

- make a planet mobile
- arrange students with labels as planets, and discuss which is closer to and farther from another
- collect round objects, such as a soccer ball and an orange, and calculate diameters and circumferences
- study each other's class schedules to determine which classes are first, second, etc.

### Unit 6: Food

Students can:

- go to a local restaurant and order lunch
- bring food and share it with the class
- introduce three typical food items from their native countries, showing an illustration to the class and/or bringing a sample
- write what they ate yesterday
- chart what they and three classmates ate yesterday
- go to a supermarket and write prices for thirty foods each includes in his or her diet
- plan and write a typical week's menu for a student in each of their native countries
- get take-out menus from three local restaurants and graph price differences for similar items
- ask a reference librarian for a book on food origins, then find and map the origins of twenty foods

## Unit 7: Maps

Students can:

- map the classroom and write instructions for going from one area to another
- map the local streets and write instructions for getting to a certain address, then exchange instructions with classmates and find the addresses
- map the local supermarket and write instructions for getting to different sections
- write questions for asking directions to the various areas, addresses, and sections they have mapped

## Unit 8: Zoo Animals

Students can:

- get a brochure from a local zoo that shows where each animal is located and make a map of the zoo
- list zoo animals in alphabetical order
- write ten questions using *where* to inquire where things are at the zoo
- write ten questions using *which* to inquire about relative size of animals

## Unit 9: Names, Addresses, and Phone Numbers

Students can:

- spell classmates' names
- graph names by number of letters
- dictate ten numbers to each other from the phone book, and check the numbers for correctness
- find ten addresses in the phone book and practice saying them with you

## Unit 10: Shapes

Students can:

- draw a design incorporating all the shapes taught in the unit
- write descriptions of their designs
- read their descriptions to you or the class
- make a mobile of shapes and label each one
- make a huge grid in the classroom and write instructions that direct classmates to each section of the grid

### Unit 11: Linear Measurement

Students can:

- measure twenty objects in the room and ask a classmate to record the length of each

- write questions about the lengths of the objects they measured

- make a chart showing the relative sizes of ten objects

### Unit 12: Liquid Measurement

Students can:

- bring containers to class and measure how much each holds

- write questions to inquire how much each container holds

- graph the relative volumes of the containers they measured

- make a chart that shows several containers, their approximate volumes, and appropriate abbreviations

### Unit 13: The Body

Students can:

- draw and label a human body

- write actions for classmates to perform

- perform actions for classmates to identify

- list five actions they each enjoy

- write a questionnaire that asks classmates to identify five favorite actions, then give the questionnaire to five classmates

- chart the results of their questionnaires

### Unit 14: Clothing

Students can:

- make a clothing catalog by cutting ads from the newspaper, labeling each item, and writing the price of each item

- name a typical item of clothing from their native countries that people in the United States don't wear, then make a poster with each student's article of clothing illustrated and labeled

- make a map of the world and note which article of clothing comes from which country

- collect clothing catalogs and complete an order form, deciding how much money they will each spend and how many items they will purchase

- chart the prices for five articles of clothing in each of their native countries and at a typical department store in the United States

## Unit 15: Musical Instruments

Students can:

- bring to class any musical instruments they can play or would like to play

- list each student's instrument or preference

- name three typical musical instruments from each of their native countries and make a classroom collage that shows everyone's instruments

# Scope and Sequence

| Unit | Listener Will Hear | Listener Will See | Listener Will Write |
|---|---|---|---|
| 1 | alphabet, American English pronunciation of U.S. and foreign cities, numbers to 100, numbers used to express temperature, numbers used to identify exercises, complete lexical streams | upper and lowercase letters, numbers to 100, Roman numerals to V, temperature expressed in writing, exercises identified by number, capitalization and punctuation in a complete sentence | upper and lowercase letters, names of U.S. and foreign cities, numbers from dictation, temperatures, complete sentences to include capitalization and punctuation |
| 2 | time expressed in hours, half hours, quarter hours, and minutes; names for daily activities; agendas; a timetable | standard clock notation, illustrations of daily activities, visual layout of an agenda, map of some U.S. cities, a bus schedule of routes connecting U.S. cities | time in numerals and clock notation, names for daily activities, dictated agenda, agenda extracted from lengthier spoken information, bus timetable |
| 3 | names for the days of the week and months of the year, number of days in each month, four calendar schedules read in the most common ways | days of the week and months of the year written in order and capitalized, typical calendar, four personal agendas | days of the week; months of the year; placement: before–after–between; number of days in each month; agendas by activity, date, and time |
| 4 | money expressed in dollars and cents, train schedule | written amounts of money, train routes: schedules and fares | notations for money, train schedule and fares |
| 5 | names of the planets, size and distance comparisons, numbers to three billion, numbers used to express distances, diameter, ordinal numbers to *ninth* | planets and their names, visual comparison of size and distances, numbers written to three billion, distances and diameter expressed in miles, ordinal numbers written to *ninth* | names of the planets, sentences comparing size and distance, numbers to three billion, distances of planets from the sun and diameter of each, ordinal numbers to *ninth* |
| 6 | names for common American foods and the three daily meals, detail of four people's menus, a supermarket price list, a week's menus, certain foods and their places of origin | illustrations and words for foods, alphabetical lists, meal menus, complete sentences telling what people eat, checklist of food preferences, supermarket price list, menu calendars, restaurant menu, map of food origins | names of foods, alphabetical lists, meal menus, sentences that tell what people eat, food preference checklist, price list, a week's menu, information from a restaurant menu, list of foods and their origins |
| 7 | directions for getting from one place to another on the street and in a supermarket | local street and supermarket maps, written directions | simple map directions |

8 names for zoo animals, locations of animals in a zoo, animal size comparisons, zoo animal origins

9 typical forms for requesting name, address, and telephone number information and for requesting clarification of same

10 names for shapes, shapes classified by number of sides, expressions for locating objects on a diagram

11 expressions for measurements in centimeters and inches, *How long* questions and answers, linear comparisons

12 words for liquid measure, *How many* and *Which is more* questions and answers, use of *full* and *empty*, liquid measure abbreviations

13 names for parts of the human body, classification of parts by extremity and upper/lower body, names for physical activities

14 names of articles of clothing, articles categorized by summer and winter wear and by length of sleeves, clothing store price list and locations, clothing contents of a suitcase

15 names of musical instruments and sections of the band or orchestra, names and places of origins of other musical instruments

---

8 illustrations and names of zoo animals, zoo map, common question forms, complete sentences to express size comparisons, map of animal origins

9 name, address, and telephone number lists, checklist of this information, sections from phone book pages

10 shapes and their names, checklist of sides of a shape, diagrams to express location

11 linear measure in inches and centimeters, notations for linear comparison

12 words for liquid measure, lists of equivalencies, illustrations of empty and full, abbreviation of liquid measure terms

13 illustrations and words for parts of the body, drawing to label, illustrations and words for activities

14 illustrations and words for articles of clothing, clothing listed by climate, sleeve length illustrated and described, clothing store ad, store map, packing list, clothing origins and map

15 illustrations and names of musical instruments, list of instruments by section in orchestra, map showing origins of instruments

---

8 names of zoo animals, zoo map interpretation, sentences to compare animal size, *Where . . . come from?* questions and answers

9 names, addresses, and telephone numbers from dictated and printed information; checklist of missing information

10 names for geometrical shapes, *How many* questions and answers, figures for shapes in a diagram from dictated instructions

11 expressions for linear measure in inches and centimeters, *How long* questions and answers, mathematical notations for linear comparisons

12 words for liquid measure, *How many* and *Which is more* questions and answers, *full* and *empty*, abbreviation of liquid units

13 words for human body parts, lists of body parts by limb and upper or lower, labels for a drawing, words for activities

14 names of articles of clothing, clothing lists by climate and sleeve length, clothing prices, simple directions to clothing store departments, *How much* questions and answers, packing lists

15 names of musical instruments, lists of instruments by section in orchestra, names of instruments and their countries of origin

Tapescript, including Reproduced Student Pages with Answers

## About This Tapescript

This tapescript includes a reproduction of each page from the student book. Answers are set off on the student pages in large, bold type. Directions, which students will hear but do not see in their books, are placed below the reproduced student pages. In some activities, the information students will hear to complete the activities follows the directions. In other activities, for example in Activity A, Letters on the facing page, small cassette logos follow the directions. In these activities, the cassette logos code the directions to the reproduced student pages and indicate the material students will hear.

Pauses between activity items have been included in the recorded material. However, since the amount of time it takes to complete an item within an activity will vary from student to student, use of the pause button is recommended whenever necessary. There is no prescribed amount of time in which students must complete an activity. In addition, some activities may require more than one listening. In other activities, students may listen to the recorded material and then complete the activity based on information given in their books.

## Unit 1: Letters and Numbers

**ACTIVITY A**                    Name _____

## Letters

**PART 1**

[1]

**A  B  C  D  E  F  G  H  I  J  K  L  M**
**a  b  c  d  e  f  g  h  i  j  k  l  m**

[2]

| ↓ A | B | C | __B__ | | I | J | K | __I__ | | I | K | M | __I__ |
|---|---|---|---|---|---|---|---|---|---|---|---|---|---|
| a | b | c | __b__ | | i | j | k | __i__ | | i | k | m | __i__ |

| B | C | D | __D__ | | J | K | L | __J__ | | B | D | F | __F__ |
|---|---|---|---|---|---|---|---|---|---|---|---|---|---|
| b | c | d | __d__ | | j | k | l | __j__ | | b | d | f | __f__ |

| C | D | E | __C__ | | K | L | M | __M__ | | D | F | H | __D__ |
|---|---|---|---|---|---|---|---|---|---|---|---|---|---|
| c | d | e | __c__ | | k | l | m | __m__ | | d | f | h | __d__ |

| D | E | F | __E__ | | A | C | E | __E__ | | F | H | J | __H__ |
|---|---|---|---|---|---|---|---|---|---|---|---|---|---|
| d | e | f | __e__ | | a | c | e | __e__ | | f | h | j | __h__ |

| E | F | G | __G__ | | C | E | G | __C__ | | H | J | L | __J__ |
|---|---|---|---|---|---|---|---|---|---|---|---|---|---|
| e | f | g | __g__ | | c | e | g | __c__ | | h | j | l | __j__ |

| F | G | H | __H__ | | H | G | I | __G__ | | J | L | A | __A__ |
|---|---|---|---|---|---|---|---|---|---|---|---|---|---|
| f | g | h | __h__ | | h | g | i | __g__ | | j | l | a | __a__ |

| H | I | J | __J__ | | G | I | K | __K__ |
|---|---|---|---|---|---|---|---|---|
| h | i | j | __j__ | | g | i | k | __k__ |

## Unit 1:  Letters and Numbers

### Activity A:  Letters

**Part 1**  *page 1*
Listen to the first half of the alphabet. Look at the capital and small letters in your book. [1]

Now you will hear groups of three letters. Listen and look at the letters in your book. You will hear one of the letters again. Write it on the line. [2]

---

*Please note that the activity title, e.g. "Letters," appears only once, at the beginning of the activity, in the Student Book. However, students will hear the title repeated on the tape before subsequent part numbers.

| | 1 |

**N O P Q R S T U V W X Y Z**
**n o p q r s t u v w x y z**

| | 2 |

| ↓ N O P **P** | V W X **W** | V X Z **Z** |
| n o p **p** | v w x **w** | v x z **z** |
| O P Q **O** | W X Y **Y** | Z O Q **Q** |
| o p q **o** | w x y **y** | z o q **q** |
| P Q R **Q** | X Y Z **Y** | O Q S **S** |
| p q r **q** | x y z **y** | o q s **s** |
| Q R S **R** | N P R **N** | Q S U **U** |
| q r s **r** | n p r **n** | q s u **u** |
| R S T **T** | P R T **T** | S U W **W** |
| r s t **t** | p r t **t** | s u w **w** |
| T U V **V** | R T V **V** | U W Y **U** |
| t u v **v** | r t v **v** | u w y **u** |
| U V W **U** | T V X **X** | |
| u v w **u** | t v x **x** | |

## Letters
### Part 2  *page 2*
Listen to the second half of the alphabet. Look at the capital and small letters in your book.  | 1 |

Now you will hear groups of three letters. Listen and look at the letters in your book. You will hear one of the letters again. Write it on the line.  | 2 |

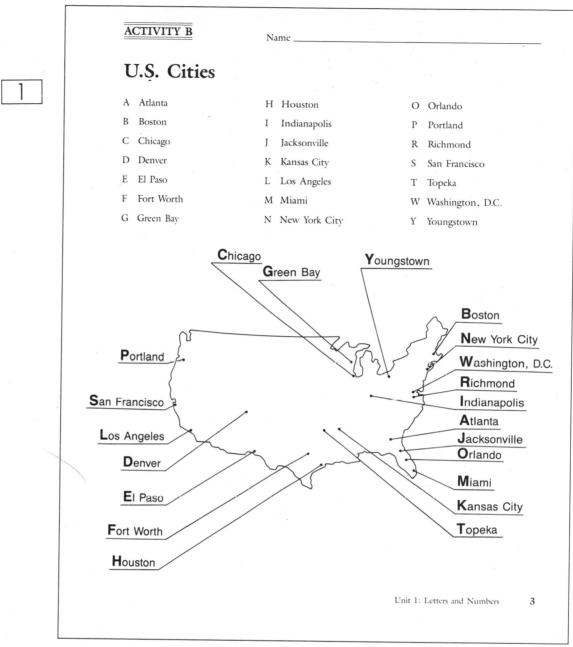

ACTIVITY B                    Name _____

# U.S. Cities

A   Atlanta          H   Houston          O   Orlando
B   Boston           I   Indianapolis     P   Portland
C   Chicago          J   Jacksonville     R   Richmond
D   Denver           K   Kansas City      S   San Francisco
E   El Paso          L   Los Angeles      T   Topeka
F   Fort Worth       M   Miami            W   Washington, D.C.
G   Green Bay        N   New York City    Y   Youngstown

Unit 1: Letters and Numbers    3

## Activity B:  U.S. Cities    *page 3*

Listen to the names of these U.S. cities. Look at them in your book. ☐1

Now find the first letter of each city on the map. Write the names of the cities on the lines.

A    Atlanta A T L A N T A
B    Boston B O S T O N
C    Chicago C H I C A G O
D    Denver D E N V E R
E    El Paso E L space P A S O
F    Fort Worth F O R T space W O R T H
G    Green Bay G R E E N space B A Y
H    Houston H O U S T O N
I    Indianapolis I N D I A N A P O L I S
J    Jacksonville J A C K S O N V I L L E

K    Kansas City K A N S A S space C I T Y
L    Los Angeles L O S space A N G E L E S
M    Miami M I A M I
N    New York City N E W space Y O R K space C I T Y
O    Orlando O R L A N D O
P    Portland P O R T L A N D
R    Richmond R I C H M O N D
S    San Francisco S A N space F R A N C I S C O
T    Topeka T O P E K A
W    Washington, D.C. W A S H I N G T O N comma D period C period
Y    Youngstown Y O U N G S T O W N

**ACTIVITY C**    Name _____

# Numbers

**PART 1**

1

2

| 1 | 2 | 3 | 4 | 5 | 6 | 7 | 8 | 9 | 10 |
|---|---|---|---|---|---|---|---|---|---|

↓ 1  2  3  __3__        2  4  5  __4__        9  8  7  __7__

2  3  4  __3__        5  3  1  __5__        10  9  8  __9__

3  4  5  __5__        5  4  2  __2__        6  8  10  __6__

3  2  1  __1__        6  7  8  __7__        7  9  10  __10__

4  3  2  __4__        7  8  9  __7__        10  8  6  __6__

5  4  3  __3__        8  9  10  __10__        10  9  7  __7__

1  3  5  __1__        8  7  6  __6__

**PART 2**

3

4

| 11 | 12 | 13 | 14 | 15 | 16 | 17 | 18 | 19 | 20 |
|----|----|----|----|----|----|----|----|----|----|

11  12  13  __11__        3  13  4  __3__        19  18  12  __12__

12  13  14  __14__        4  14  5  __14__        20  19  18  __20__

13  14  15  __15__        5  15  1  __15__        6  16  7  __7__

13  12  11  __11__        16  17  18  __18__        7  17  8  __17__

14  13  12  __13__        17  18  19  __17__        8  18  9  __9__

15  14  13  __15__        18  19  20  __20__        9  19  10  __19__

1  11  2  __2__        18  17  16  __16__        10  20  6  __20__

2  12  3  __12__

## Activity C: Numbers

**Part 1**  *page 4*
Listen to these numbers. Look at them in your book.    1

Now you will hear groups of three numbers. Listen
and look at the numbers in your book. You will hear    2
one of the numbers again. Write it on the line.

**Numbers**
**Part 2**  *page 4*
Listen to these numbers. Look at them in your book.    3

Now you will hear groups of three numbers. Listen
and look at the numbers in your book. You will hear
one of the numbers again. Write it on the line.    4

Name _____

# More Numbers

**PART 1**

**20   30   40   50   60   70   80   90   100**

| | | | | | | | | | | | | |
|---|---|---|---|---|---|---|---|---|---|---|---|---|
| 20 | 30 | 40 | **30** | 2 | 12 | 20 | **12** | 100 | 90 | 80 | **90** |
| 30 | 40 | 50 | **50** | 3 | 13 | 30 | **30** | 16 | 60 | 17 | **17** |
| 40 | 50 | 60 | **40** | 4 | 14 | 40 | **14** | 17 | 70 | 18 | **18** |
| 40 | 30 | 20 | **30** | 5 | 15 | 50 | **15** | 18 | 80 | 19 | **18** |
| 50 | 40 | 30 | **40** | 1 | 10 | 11 | **10** | 19 | 90 | 16 | **16** |
| 60 | 50 | 40 | **60** | 60 | 70 | 80 | **60** | 6 | 16 | 60 | **6** |
| 12 | 20 | 2 | **12** | 70 | 80 | 90 | **90** | 7 | 17 | 70 | **17** |
| 13 | 30 | 14 | **30** | 80 | 90 | 100 | **100** | 8 | 18 | 80 | **80** |
| 14 | 40 | 15 | **40** | 80 | 70 | 60 | **70** | 9 | 19 | 90 | **90** |
| 15 | 50 | 11 | **15** | 90 | 80 | 70 | **70** | 1 | 10 | 100 | **10** |

**PART 2**

**21   32   43   54   65   76   87   98**

| | | | | |
|---|---|---|---|---|
| 22 | 62 | 84 | 95 | 67 |
| 33 | 72 | 94 | 26 | 78 |
| 44 | 82 | 34 | 88 | 88 |
| 21 | 92 | 44 | 99 | 98 |
| 31 | 23 | 54 | 80 | 29 |
| 41 | 55 | 65 | 36 | 39 |
| 51 | 66 | 75 | 46 | 49 |
| 52 | 77 | 85 | 57 | |

## Activity D:  More Numbers

**Part 1**  *page 5*
Listen to these numbers. Look at them in your book.

Now you will hear groups of three numbers. Listen and look at the numbers in your book. You will hear one of the numbers again. Write it on the line.

**More Numbers**
**Part 2**  *page 5*
Listen to these numbers. Look at them in your book. Then listen and write the numbers on the lines in your book.

1

(Students will hear the name of each city and the Fahrenheit and Centigrade temperature only one time.)

## ACTIVITY E

Name _____

# Temperatures

| | | | | | | |
|---|---|---|---|---|---|---|
| 1. | Atlanta | 86°F | 30°C | Atlanta | 86°F | 30°C |
| 2. | Boston | 86°F | 30°C | Boston | 86°F | 30°C |
| 3. | Chicago | 89°F | 32°C | Chicago | 89°F | 32°C |
| 4. | Denver | 81°F | 27°C | Denver | 81°F | 27°C |
| 5. | El Paso | 98°F | 37°C | El Paso | 98°F | 37°C |
| 6. | Fort Worth | 93°F | 34°C | Fort Worth | 93°F | 34°C |
| 7. | Green Bay | 83°F | 28°C | Green Bay | 83°F | 28°C |
| 8. | Houston | 90°F | 32°C | Houston | 90°F | 32°C |
| 9. | Indianapolis | 87°F | 31°C | Indianapolis | 87°F | 31°C |
| 10. | Jacksonville | 94°F | 34°C | Jacksonville | 94°F | 34°C |
| 11. | Kansas City | 86°F | 30°C | Kansas City | 86°F | 30°C |
| 12. | Los Angeles | 79°F | 26°C | Los Angeles | 79°F | 26°C |
| 13. | Miami | 86°F | 30°C | Miami | 86°F | 30°C |
| 14. | New York City | 90°F | 32°C | New York City | 90°F | 32°C |
| 15. | Orlando | 97°F | 36°C | Orlando | 97°F | 36°C |
| 16. | Portland | 82°F | 28°C | Portland | 82°F | 28°C |
| 17. | Richmond | 89°F | 32°C | Richmond | 89°F | 32°C |
| 18. | San Francisco | 65°F | 18°C | San Francisco | 65°F | 18°C |
| 19. | Topeka | 87°F | 31°C | Topeka | 87°F | 31°C |
| 20. | Washington, D.C. | 89°F | 32°C | Washington, D.C. | 89°F | 32°C |
| 21. | Youngstown | 91°F | 33°C | Youngstown | 91°F | 33°C |

## Activity E: Temperatures *page 6*

Listen to the cities and their temperatures. You will hear each temperature in both Fahrenheit and Centigrade. Write the temperatures on the lines in your book.

1

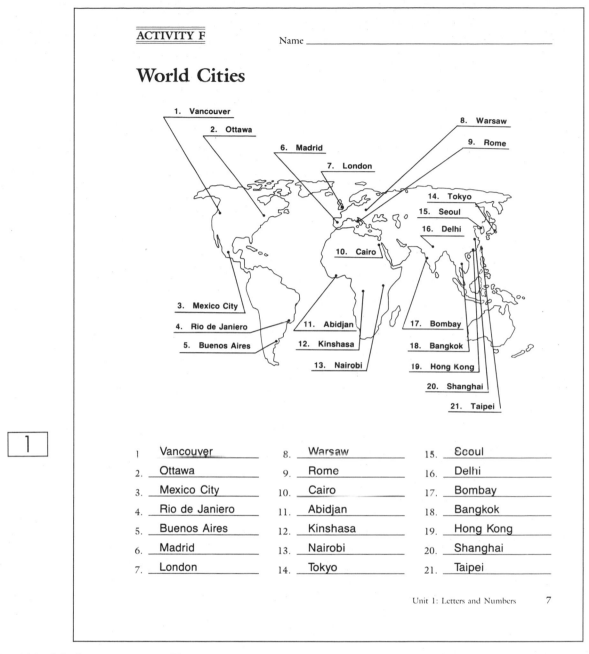

Name _____

# World Cities

1. Vancouver
2. Ottawa
6. Madrid
7. London
8. Warsaw
9. Rome
14. Tokyo
15. Seoul
16. Delhi
10. Cairo
3. Mexico City
4. Rio de Janiero
5. Buenos Aires
11. Abidjan
12. Kinshasa
13. Nairobi
17. Bombay
18. Bangkok
19. Hong Kong
20. Shanghai
21. Taipei

1

| | | |
|---|---|---|
| 1. Vancouver | 8. Warsaw | 15. Seoul |
| 2. Ottawa | 9. Rome | 16. Delhi |
| 3. Mexico City | 10. Cairo | 17. Bombay |
| 4. Rio de Janiero | 11. Abidjan | 18. Bangkok |
| 5. Buenos Aires | 12. Kinshasa | 19. Hong Kong |
| 6. Madrid | 13. Nairobi | 20. Shanghai |
| 7. London | 14. Tokyo | 21. Taipei |

## Activity F:  World Cities   *page 7*

Listen to the names of these cities and write them on the lines in your book. Look at the map if you need help.   1

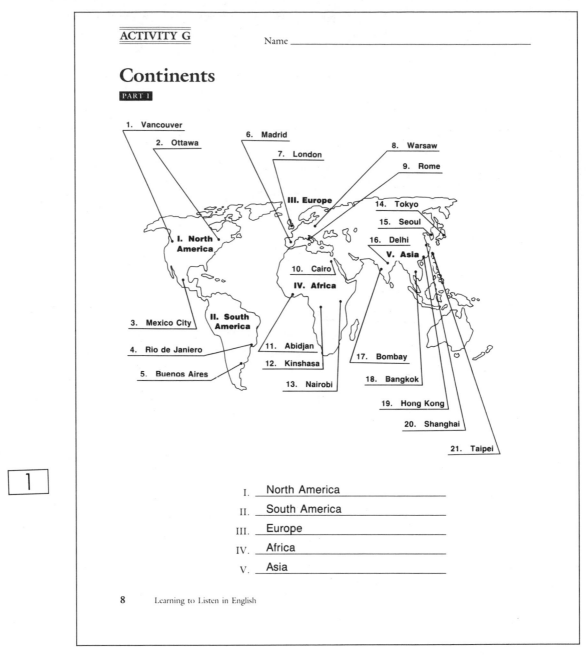

# Continents
**PART 1**

1. Vancouver
2. Ottawa
6. Madrid
7. London
8. Warsaw
9. Rome
**III. Europe**
14. Tokyo
15. Seoul
16. Delhi
**V. Asia**
**I. North America**
10. Cairo
**IV. Africa**
3. Mexico City
**II. South America**
4. Rio de Janiero
5. Buenos Aires
11. Abidjan
12. Kinshasa
13. Nairobi
17. Bombay
18. Bangkok
19. Hong Kong
20. Shanghai
21. Taipei

1

I. North America _____
II. South America _____
III. Europe _____
IV. Africa _____
V. Asia _____

## Activity G: Continents

**Part 1** *page 8*
Listen to the names of these continents and write them on the lines in your book. Look at the map if you need help.    1

1

**PART 2**                    Name _____

**North America**

1. Vancouver
2. Ottawa
3. Mexico City

**South America**

4. Rio de Janiero
5. Buenos Aires

**Europe**

6. Madrid
7. London
8. Warsaw
9. Rome

**Africa**

10. Cairo
11. Abidjan
12. Kinshasa
13. Nairobi

**Asia**

14. Tokyo
15. Seoul
16. Delhi
17. Bombay
18. Bangkok
19. Hong Kong
20. Shanghai
21. Taipei

**Continents**

**Part 2**  *page 9*

Listen to the names of these cities. Write them on the lines under the correct continents. Look at the map on page 8 if you need help.

1

1

ACTIVITY H          Name _____

# Cities and Continents

1. Vancouver is in North America. _____
2. Ottawa is in North America. _____
3. Mexico City is in North America. _____
4. Rio de Janiero is in South America. _____
5. Buenos Aires is in South America. _____
6. Madrid is in Europe. _____
7. London is in Europe. _____
8. Warsaw is in Europe. _____
9. Rome is in Europe. _____
10. Cairo is in Africa. _____
11. Abidjan is in Africa. _____
12. Kinshasa is in Africa. _____
13. Nairobi is in Africa. _____
14. Tokyo is in Asia. _____
15. Seoul is in Asia. _____
16. Delhi is in Asia. _____
17. Bombay is in Asia. _____
18. Bangkok is in Asia. _____
19. Hong Kong is in Asia. _____
20. Shanghai is in Asia. _____
21. Taipei is in Asia. _____

## Activity H:  Cities and Continents
*page 10*

Listen to the sentences and write them in your book.   1

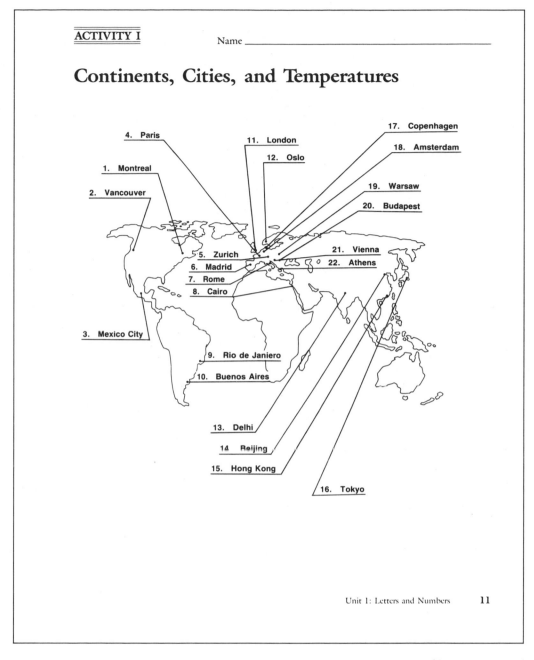

(See page 12.)

1

| | Continent | City | Temperature |
|---|---|---|---|
| 1. | North America | Montreal | 91°F |
| 2. | North America | Vancouver | 78°F |
| 3. | North America | Mexico City | 79°F |
| 4. | Europe | Paris | 86°F |
| 5. | Europe | Zurich | 82°F |
| 6. | Europe | Madrid | 97°F |
| 7. | Europe | Rome | 90°F |
| 8. | Africa | Cairo | 93°F |
| 9. | South America | Rio de Janiero | 84°F |
| 10. | South America | Buenos Aires | 68°F |
| 11. | Europe | London | 72°F |
| 12. | Europe | Oslo | 66°F |
| 13. | Asia | Delhi | 100°F |
| 14. | Asia | Beijing | 93°F |
| 15. | Asia | Hong Kong | 91°F |
| 16. | Asia | Tokyo | 81°F |
| 17. | Europe | Copenhagen | 61°F |
| 18. | Europe | Amsterdam | 70°F |
| 19. | Europe | Warsaw | 67°F |
| 20. | Europe | Budapest | 74°F |
| 21. | Europe | Vienna | 81°F |
| 22. | Europe | Athens | 90°F |

## Activity 1: Continents, Cities, and Temperatures *pages 11 and 12*

Listen to these continents, cities, and temperatures. Write them in your book. Look at the map on page 11 if you need help.  1

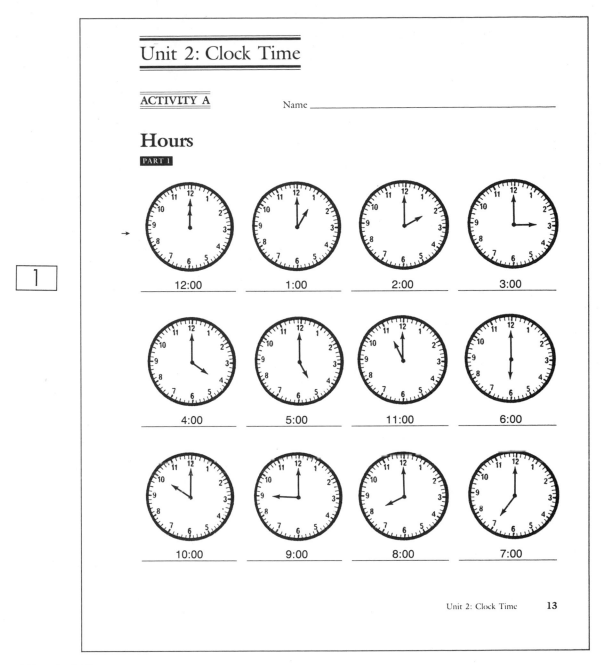

# Unit 2: Clock Time

## Unit 2:  Clock Time

### Activity A:  Hours

**Part 1**  *page 13*
Listen to the times and look at the clocks in your book.
Write the correct time on the line by each clock.

1

PART 2                    Name _____

1

| | | | |
|---|---|---|---|
| 12:00 | 1:00 | 2:00 | 3:00 |
| 4:00 | 5:00 | 11:00 | 6:00 |
| 10:00 | 9:00 | 8:00 | 7:00 |

(Students should also have drawn hands on these clocks to show the correct times. The student-drawn hands should show the same times as the clocks in Part 1 of this activity.)

**Hours**
**Part 2**  *page 14*
Listen to the times and write them in your book. Then draw hands on each clock to show the correct time.  1

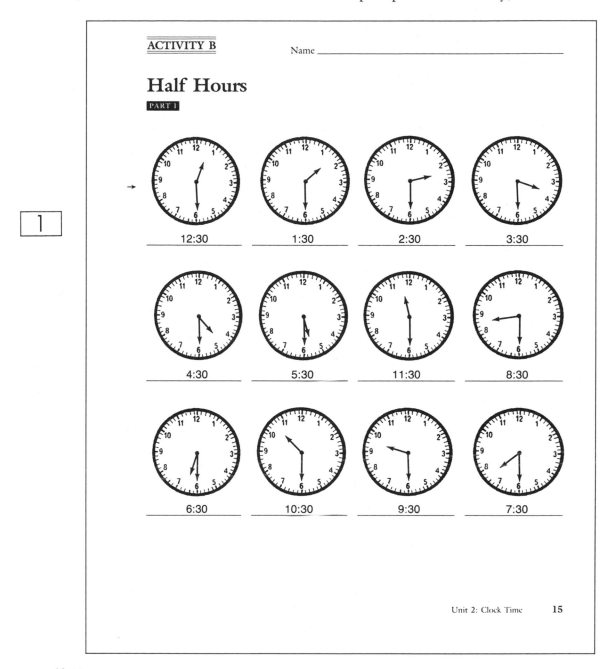

1

**ACTIVITY B**                    Name _____

# Half Hours

**PART 1**

| | | | |
|---|---|---|---|
| 12:30 | 1:30 | 2:30 | 3:30 |
| 4:30 | 5:30 | 11:30 | 8:30 |
| 6:30 | 10:30 | 9:30 | 7:30 |

Unit 2: Clock Time    15

## Activity B:  Half Hours

**Part 1** *page 15*

Listen to the times and look at the clocks in your book.
Write the correct time on the line by each clock.    1

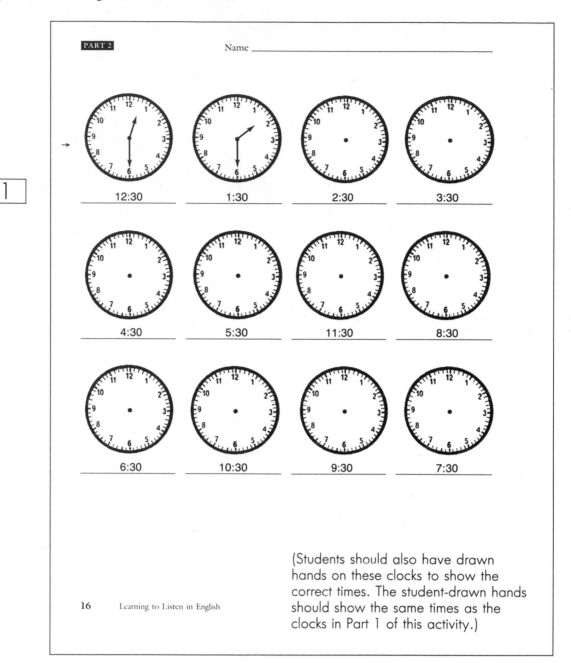

PART 2          Name _____

1

12:30          1:30          2:30          3:30

4:30          5:30          11:30          8:30

6:30          10:30          9:30          7:30

(Students should also have drawn hands on these clocks to show the correct times. The student-drawn hands should show the same times as the clocks in Part 1 of this activity.)

16      Learning to Listen in English

## Half Hours
### Part 2   page 16
Listen to the times and write them in your book. Then draw hands on each clock to show the correct time.    1

ACTIVITY C    Name _____

# Quarter Hours
PART 1

**1**

| 12:15 | 1:15 | 2:15 | 11:15 |

| 10:15 | 7:15 | 5:15 | 4:15 |

| 6:15 | 8:15 | 9:15 | 3:15 |

Unit 2: Clock Time    **17**

## Activity C: Quarter Hours*

**Part 1**  *page 17*

Listen to the times and look at the clocks in your book.
Write the correct time on the line by each clock.    **1**

*Students will hear and practice both types of time expressions for quarter hours, i.e., "twelve fifteen" and "a quarter past twelve," and twelve forty-five and a quarter to one," because they will encounter both expressions in the course of daily life.

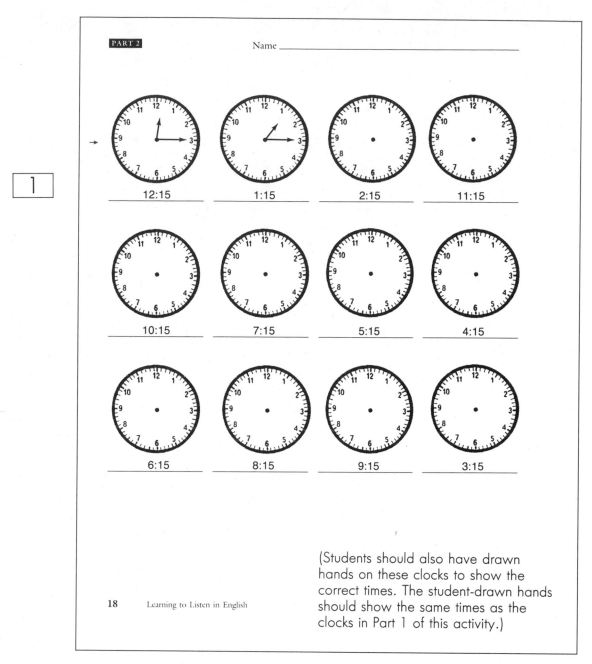

1

12:15    1:15    2:15    11:15

10:15    7:15    5:15    4:15

6:15    8:15    9:15    3:15

(Students should also have drawn hands on these clocks to show the correct times. The student-drawn hands should show the same times as the clocks in Part 1 of this activity.)

## Quarter Hours
**Part 2**  *page 18*

Listen to the times and write them in your book. Then draw hands on each clock to show the correct time.    | 1 |

ACTIVITY D

Name _____

# More Quarter Hours
PART 1

| | | | |
|---|---|---|---|
| 12:45 | 1:45 | 2:45 | 6:45 |
| 8:45 | 10:45 | 11:45 | 9:45 |
| 7:45 | 5:45 | 3:45 | 4:45 |

1

## Activity D:  More Quarter Hours

**Part 1**  *page 19*
Listen to the times and look at the clocks in your book.
Write the correct time on the line by each clock.    1

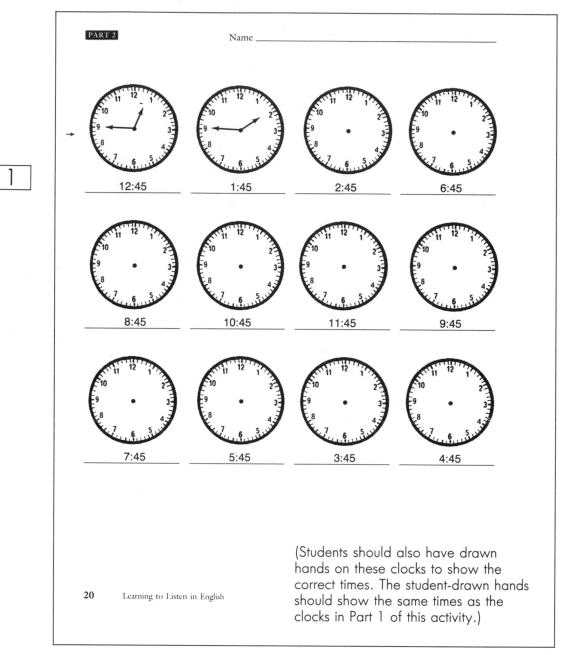

(Students should also have drawn hands on these clocks to show the correct times. The student-drawn hands should show the same times as the clocks in Part 1 of this activity.)

## More Quarter Hours
**Part 2**  *page 20*

Listen to the times and write them in your book. Then draw hands on each clock to show the correct time.  1

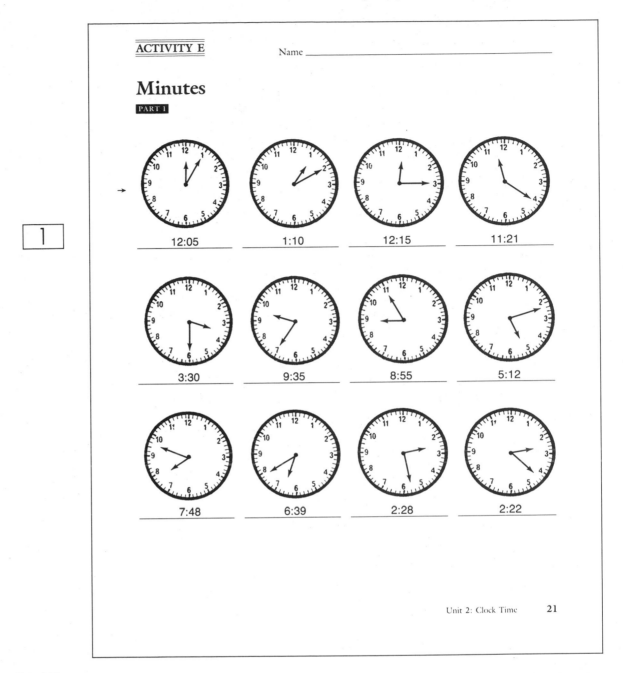

ACTIVITY E          Name _____

# Minutes
PART 1

| | | | |
|---|---|---|---|
| 12:05 | 1:10 | 12:15 | 11:21 |
| 3:30 | 9:35 | 8:55 | 5:12 |
| 7:48 | 6:39 | 2:28 | 2:22 |

Unit 2: Clock Time    21

## Activity E: Minutes

**Part 1**  *page 21*
Listen to the times and look at the clocks in your book.
Write the correct time on the line by each clock.   1

PART 2                    Name _____

1

12:05              1:10              12:15              11:21

3:30              9:35              8:55              5:12

7:48              6:39              2:28              2:22

(Students should also have drawn
hands on these clocks to show the
correct times. The student-drawn hands
should show the same times as the
clocks in Part 1 of this activity.)

22        Learning to Listen in English

**Minutes**
**Part 2**  *page 22*
Listen to the times and write them in your book. Then
draw hands on each clock to show the correct time.       1

ACTIVITY F                    Name _____

# Writing the Time

1
|     |        |     |         |
|-----|--------|-----|---------|
| 1.  | 1:00   | 21. | 11:15   |
| 2.  | 2:15   | 22. | 11:10   |
| 3.  | 3:30   | 23. | 12:35   |
| 4.  | 4:25   | 24. | 12:05   |
| 5.  | 5:50   | 25. | 8:15    |
| 6.  | 6:30   | 26. | 7:45    |
| 7.  | 7:15   | 27. | 3:15    |
| 8.  | 2:45   | 28. | 1:15    |
| 9.  | 6:20   | 29. | 1:35    |
| 10. | 7:10   | 30. | 2:25    |
| 11. | 8:45   | 31. | 2:40    |
| 12. | 10:45  | 32. | 3:15    |
| 13. | 11:05  | 33. | 4:15    |
| 14. | 12:30  | 34. | 4:25    |
| 15. | 12:15  | 35. | 4:50    |
| 16. | 11:25  | 36. | 5:15    |
| 17. | 10:10  | 37. | 6:05    |
| 18. | 12:15  | 38. | 6:45    |
| 19. | 10:40  | 39. | 7:20    |
| 20. | 10:20  | 40. | 8:55    |

## Activity F:  Writing the Time   *page 23*    1

Listen to these times and write them in your book.   1

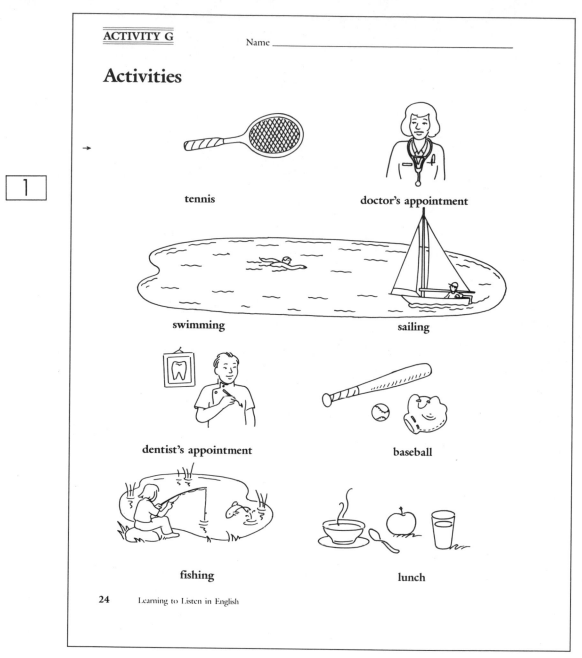

**ACTIVITY G**          Name _____

## Activities

1

tennis

doctor's appointment

swimming

sailing

dentist's appointment

baseball

fishing

lunch

## Activity G: Activities  *page 24*

Listen to the names of these activities. Look at the
words and pictures in your book.  1

ACTIVITY H    Name _____

# Agenda

| | |
|---|---|
| 8:00 | fishing _____ |
| 8:30 | _____ |
| 9:00 | _____ |
| 9:30 | dentist's appointment _____ |
| 10:00 | _____ |
| 10:30 | _____ |
| 11:00 | baseball _____ |
| 11:30 | _____ |
| 12:00 | _____ |
| 12:30 | lunch _____ |
| 1:00 | _____ |
| 1:30 | _____ |
| 2:00 | _____ |
| 2:30 | sailing _____ |
| 3:00 | _____ |
| 3:30 | _____ |
| 4:00 | _____ |
| 4:30 | _____ |
| 5:00 | tennis _____ |

## Activity H: Agenda  *page 25*

Listen to this agenda. Write each activity on the line
by the correct time. You will not write on every line.

    8:00, fishing
    9:30, dentist's appointment
    11:00, baseball
    12:30, lunch
    2:30, sailing
    5:00, tennis

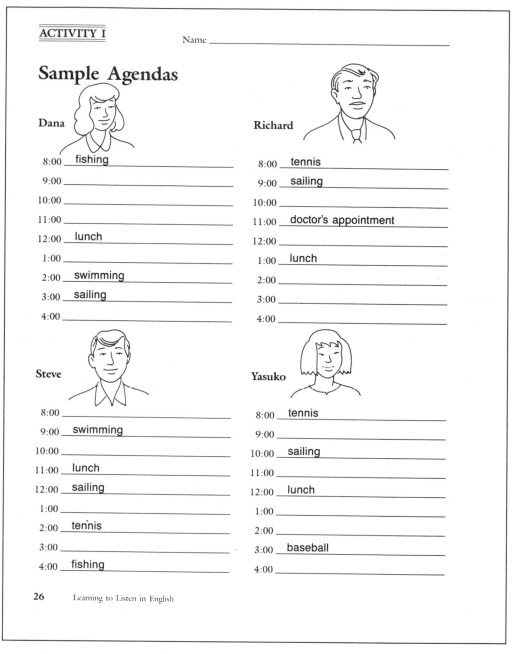

ACTIVITY I                    Name _____

## Sample Agendas

**Dana**

8:00 ___fishing___
9:00 _____
10:00 _____
11:00 _____
12:00 ___lunch___
1:00 _____
2:00 ___swimming___
3:00 ___sailing___
4:00 _____

**Richard**

8:00 ___tennis___
9:00 ___sailing___
10:00 _____
11:00 ___doctor's appointment___
12:00 _____
1:00 ___lunch___
2:00 _____
3:00 _____
4:00 _____

**Steve**

8:00 _____
9:00 ___swimming___
10:00 _____
11:00 ___lunch___
12:00 ___sailing___
1:00 _____
2:00 ___tennis___
3:00 _____
4:00 ___fishing___

**Yasuko**

8:00 ___tennis___
9:00 _____
10:00 ___sailing___
11:00 _____
12:00 ___lunch___
1:00 _____
2:00 _____
3:00 ___baseball___
4:00 _____

26    Learning to Listen in English

## Activity I:  Sample Agendas  *page 26*

Listen to these agendas for Dana, Richard, Steve, and Yasuko. Write each activity on the line by the correct time. You will not write on every line.

Dana:    8:00, fishing        Richard:    8:00, tennis
         12:00, lunch                     9:00, sailing
         2:00, swimming                   11:00, doctor's appointment
         3:00, sailing                    1:00, lunch

Steve:   9:00, swimming       Yasuko:    8:00, tennis
         11:00, lunch                     10:00, sailing
         12:00, sailing                   12:00, lunch
         2:00, tennis                     3:00, baseball
         4:00, fishing

ACTIVITY J

Name _____

# More Agendas

|  |  | Activity | Time |
|---|---|---|---|
| Dana: | 1. | fishing | 7:00 |
|  | 2. | lunch | 12:00 |
|  | 3. | sailing | 2:00 |
|  | 4. | baseball | 4:00 |
| Richard: | 5. | doctor's appointment | 8:00 |
|  | 6. | tennis | 10:00 |
|  | 7. | lunch | 1:00 |
|  | 8. | baseball | 4:00 |
| Steve: | 9. | fishing | 8:00 |
|  | 10. | dentist's appointment | 10:00 |
|  | 11. | tennis | 11:00 |
|  | 12. | lunch | 1:00 |
| Yasuko: | 13. | baseball | 7:00 |
|  | 14. | sailing | 10:00 |
|  | 15. | lunch | 11:00 |
|  | 16. | tennis | 4:00 |

## Activity J: More Agendas  page 27

Listen to these agendas. Write the activities and the times on the lines in your book.

1. Dana goes fishing at 7:00.
2. She eats lunch at 12:00.
3. She goes sailing at 2:00.
4. She plays baseball at 4:00.
5. Richard has a doctor's appointment at 8:00.
6. He plays tennis at 10:00.
7. He has lunch at 1:00.
8. He plays baseball at 4:00.
9. Steve goes fishing at 8:00.
10. His dentist's appointment is at 10:00.
11. He plays tennis at 11:00.
12. He has lunch at 1:00.
13. Yasuko plays baseball at 7:00.
14. She goes sailing at 10:00.
15. She has lunch at 11:00.
16. She plays tennis at 4:00.

<u>ACTIVITY K</u>    Name _____

# Bus Timetable 1

| Leaving | | Arriving | |
|---|---|---|---|
| Albuquerque | 12:00 | Denver | 8:15 |
| Atlanta | 1:00 | New Orleans | 11:05 |
| Boston | 2:30 | New York City | 7:45 |
| Chicago | 3:45 | Cleveland | 11:00 |
| Los Angeles | 4:15 | San Francisco | 1:45 |
| New York City | 5:00 | Washington, D.C. | 10:30 |

## Activity K:  Bus Timetable 1  *page 28*

Listen to this bus timetable and look at it in your book.

   Leaving Albuquerque at 12:00, arriving Denver at 8:15.

   Leaving Atlanta at 1:00, arriving New Orleans at 11:05.

   Leaving Boston at 2:30, arriving New York City at 7:45.

   Leaving Chicago at 3:45, arriving Cleveland at 11:00.

   Leaving Los Angeles at 4:15, arriving San Francisco at 1:45.

   Leaving New York City at 5:00, arriving Washington, D.C. at 10:30.

## ACTIVITY L

Name _____

# Bus Timetable 2

| | Leaving | | Arriving | |
|---|---|---|---|---|
| 1. | Albuquerque | 2:00 | Los Angeles | 5:00 |
| 2. | Albuquerque | 3:15 | San Francisco | 6:45 |
| 3. | Atlanta | 12:00 | Chicago | 5:15 |
| 4. | Atlanta | 1:00 | Cleveland | 7:50 |
| 5. | Boston | 6:45 | New York City | 11:45 |
| 6. | Boston | 8:00 | Washington, D.C. | 6:15 |
| 7. | Chicago | 2:15 | Cleveland | 9:30 |
| 8. | Chicago | 12:00 | New Orleans | 10:30 |
| 9. | Cleveland | 7:00 | Chicago | 2:25 |
| 10. | Cleveland | 9:30 | New York City | 7:45 |
| 11. | Denver | 10:45 | Albuquerque | 7:00 |
| 12. | Denver | 11:15 | Los Angeles | 9:45 |
| 13. | Los Angeles | 1:45 | Albuquerque | 9:00 |
| 14. | Los Angeles | 12:30 | San Francisco | 9:30 |
| 15. | New York City | 2:15 | Boston | 6:45 |
| 16. | New York City | 3:00 | Washington, D.C. | 8:45 |
| 17. | New Orleans | 4:25 | Atlanta | 2:45 |
| 18. | New Orleans | 3:15 | Albuquerque | 2:10 |
| 19. | San Francisco | 8:00 | Los Angeles | 5:00 |
| 20. | San Francisco | 12:30 | Albuquerque | 12:30 |
| 21. | Washington, D.C. | 6:20 | Boston | 4:15 |
| 22. | Washington, D.C. | 8:45 | Cleveland | 5:15 |

Unit 2: Clock Time    29

## Activity L: Bus Timetable 2
*page 29*

Listen to this bus timetable. Write the cities and times in the "leaving" and "arriving" columns in your workbook.

1. Leaving Albuquerque, 2:00, arriving Los Angeles, 5:00.
2. Leaving Albuquerque, 3:15, arriving San Francisco, 6:45.
3. Leaving Atlanta, 12:00, arriving Chicago, 5:15.
4. Leaving Atlanta, 1:00, arriving Cleveland, 7:50.
5. Leaving Boston, 6:45, arriving New York City, 11:45.
6. Leaving Boston, 8:00, arriving Washington, D.C., 6:15.
7. Leaving Chicago, 2:15, arriving Cleveland, 9:30.
8. Leaving Chicago, 12:00, arriving New Orleans, 10:30.
9. Leaving Cleveland, 7:00, arriving Chicago, 2:25.
10. Leaving Cleveland, 9:30, arriving New York City, 7:45.
11. Leaving Denver, 10:45, arriving Albuquerque, 7:00.
12. Leaving Denver, 11:15, arriving Los Angeles, 9:45.
13. Leaving Los Angeles, 1:45, arriving Albuquerque, 9:00.
14. Leaving Los Angeles, 12:30, arriving San Francisco, 9:30.
15. Leaving New York City, 2:15, arriving Boston, 6:45.
16. Leaving New York City, 3:00, arriving Washington, D.C., 8:45.
17. Leaving New Orleans, 4:25, arriving Atlanta, 2:45.
18. Leaving New Orleans, 3:15, arriving Albuquerque, 2:10.
19. Leaving San Francisco, 8:00, arriving Los Angeles, 5:00.
20. Leaving San Francisco, 12:30, arriving Albuquerque, 12:30.
21. Leaving Washington, D.C., 6:20, arriving Boston, 4:15.
22. Leaving Washington, D.C., 8:45, arriving Cleveland, 5:15.

## Unit 3: Calendar Time

ACTIVITY A                  Name _____

# Days of the Week

PART 1

1

2

(Students will hear each day of the week only one time.)

| Sunday | Monday | Tuesday | Wednesday | Thursday | Friday | Saturday |
|--------|--------|---------|-----------|----------|--------|----------|

1. Sunday     _Sunday_
2. Monday     _Monday_
3. Tuesday     _Tuesday_
4. Wednesday     _Wednesday_
5. Thursday     _Thursday_
6. Friday     _Friday_
7. Saturday     _Saturday_

3

PART 2

| Sunday | _Monday_ | Tuesday |
| Monday | _Tuesday_ | Wednesday |
| Tuesday | _Wednesday_ | Thursday |
| Wednesday | _Thursday_ | Friday |
| Thursday | _Friday_ | Saturday |
| Friday | _Saturday_ | Sunday |
| Saturday | _Sunday_ | Monday |

## Unit 3: Calendar Time

### Activity A: Days of the Week

**Part 1** *page 30*
Listen to the days of the week and look at them in your book.

1

Now listen to the days of the week again and write them in your book.

2

**Days of the Week**
**Part 2** *page 30*
You will hear groups of three days. Listen and write the day that comes *between* the two days in your book.

3

# Days of the Week with <u>After</u>, <u>Before</u>, and <u>Between</u>

**PART 1**

| after | | |
|---|---|---|
| | Saturday | Sunday |
| | Sunday | Monday |
| | Monday | Tuesday |
| | Tuesday | Wednesday |
| | Wednesday | Thursday |
| | Thursday | Friday |
| | Friday | Saturday |

**PART 2**

| before | | |
|---|---|---|
| | Saturday | Sunday |
| | Sunday | Monday |
| | Monday | Tuesday |
| | Tuesday | Wednesday |
| | Wednesday | Thursday |
| | Thursday | Friday |
| | Friday | Saturday |

**PART 3**

| between | | | |
|---|---|---|---|
| | Saturday | Sunday | Monday |
| | Tuesday | Wednesday | Thursday |
| | Friday | Saturday | Sunday |
| | Monday | Tuesday | Wednesday |
| | Thursday | Friday | Saturday |
| | Wednesday | Thursday | Friday |
| | Sunday | Monday | Tuesday |

Unit 3: Calendar Time    **31**

## Activity B: Days of the Week with *After, Before,* and *Between*

**Part 1**  *page 31*
Listen to the sentences. Write the day that comes *after* each day in your book.

The day after Saturday is Sunday.
The day after Sunday is Monday.
The day after Monday is Tuesday.
The day after Tuesday is Wednesday.
The day after Wednesday is Thursday.
The day after Thursday is Friday.
The day after Friday is Saturday.

**Days of the Week**
**Part 2**  *page 31*
Listen to the sentences. Write the day that comes *before* each day in your book.

The day before Sunday is Saturday.
The day before Monday is Sunday.
The day before Tuesday is Monday.
The day before Wednesday is Tuesday.
The day before Thursday is Wednesday.
The day before Friday is Thursday.
The day before Saturday is Friday.

**Days of the Week**
**Part 3**  *page 31*
Listen to the sentences. Write the day that comes *between* the two days in your book.

The day between Saturday and Monday is Sunday.
The day between Tuesday and Thursday is Wednesday.
The day between Friday and Sunday is Saturday.
The day between Monday and Wednesday is Tuesday.
The day between Thursday and Saturday is Friday.
The day between Wednesday and Friday is Thursday.
The day between Sunday and Tuesday is Monday.

(Students will hear each month of the year only one time.)

---

**ACTIVITY C**    Name _____

# Months of the Year

**PART 1**

| January | February | March | April | May | June |
| July | August | September | October | November | December |

| | | | | |
|---|---|---|---|---|
| 1. January | January | 7. July | July |
| 2. February | February | 8. August | August |
| 3. March | March | 9. September | September |
| 4. April | April | 10. October | October |
| 5. May | May | 11. November | November |
| 6. June | June | 12. December | December |

**PART 2**

| | | | |
|---|---|---|---|
| January | February | March | |
| February | March | April | |
| March | April | May | |
| April | May | June | |
| May | June | July | |
| June | July | August | |
| July | August | September | |
| August | September | October | |
| September | October | November | |
| October | November | December | |

---

## Activity C: Months of the Year

**Part 1**  *page 32*
Listen to the months of the year and look at them in your book.

Now listen to the months of the year again and write them in your book.

**Months of the Year**
**Part 2**  *page 32*
You will hear groups of three months. Listen and write the month that comes *between* the two months in your book.

Name _____

# Months of the Year with <u>After</u>, <u>Before</u>, and <u>Between</u>

**PART 1**

after

| | |
|---|---|
| January | February |
| February | March |
| April | May |
| June | July |
| August | September |
| November | December |

**PART 2**

before

| | |
|---|---|
| March | April |
| January | February |
| October | November |
| May | June |
| July | August |
| December | January |

**PART 3**

between

| | | |
|---|---|---|
| January | February | March |
| May | June | July |
| September | October | November |
| April | May | June |

Unit 3: Calendar Time    **33**

## Activity D: Months of the Year with *After, Before,* and *Between*

**Part 1** *page 33*
Listen to the sentences. Write the month that comes *after* each month in your book.

The month after January is February.
The month after February is March.
The month after April is May.
The month after June is July.
The month after August is September.
The month after November is December.

**Months of the Year**
**Part 2** *page 33*
Listen to the sentences. Write the month that comes *before* each month in your book.

The month before April is March.

The month before February is January.

The month before November is October.

The month before June is May.

The month before August is July.

The month before January is December.

**Months of the Year**
**Part 3** *page 33*
Listen to the sentences. Write the month that comes *between* the two months in your book.

The month between January and March is February.

The month between May and July is June.

The month between September and November is October.

The month between April and June is May.

## ACTIVITY E

Name _____

# The Calendar

| January | February | March | April |
|---------|----------|-------|-------|
| S M T W T F S | S M T W T F S | S M T W T F S | S M T W T F S |
| 1 2 | 1 2 3 4 5 6 | 1 2 3 4 5 | 1 2 |
| 3 4 5 6 7 8 9 | 7 8 9 10 11 12 13 | 6 7 8 9 10 11 12 | 3 4 5 6 7 8 9 |
| 10 11 12 13 14 15 16 | 14 15 16 17 18 19 20 | 13 14 15 16 17 18 19 | 10 11 12 13 14 15 16 |
| 17 18 19 20 21 22 23 | 21 22 23 24 25 26 27 | 20 21 22 23 24 25 26 | 17 18 19 20 21 22 23 |
| 24 25 26 27 28 29 30 | 28 29 | 27 28 29 30 31 | 24 25 26 27 28 29 30 |
| 31 | | | |

| May | June | July | August |
|-----|------|------|--------|
| S M T W T F S | S M T W T F S | S M T W T F S | S M T W T F S |
| 1 2 3 4 5 6 7 | 1 2 3 4 | 1 2 | 1 2 3 4 5 6 |
| 8 9 10 11 12 13 14 | 5 6 7 8 9 10 11 | 3 4 5 6 7 8 9 | 7 8 9 10 11 12 13 |
| 15 16 17 18 19 20 21 | 12 13 14 15 16 17 18 | 10 11 12 13 14 15 16 | 14 15 16 17 18 19 20 |
| 22 23 24 25 26 27 28 | 19 20 21 22 23 24 25 | 17 18 19 20 21 22 23 | 21 22 23 24 25 26 27 |
| 29 30 31 | 26 27 28 29 30 | 24 25 26 27 28 29 30 | 28 29 30 31 |
| | | 31 | |

| September | October | November | December |
|-----------|---------|----------|----------|
| S M T W T F S | S M T W T F S | S M T W T F S | S M T W T F S |
| 1 2 3 | 1 | 1 2 3 4 5 | 1 2 3 |
| 4 5 6 7 8 9 10 | 2 3 4 5 6 7 8 | 6 7 8 9 10 11 12 | 4 5 6 7 8 9 10 |
| 11 12 13 14 15 16 17 | 9 10 11 12 13 14 15 | 13 14 15 16 17 18 19 | 11 12 13 14 15 16 17 |
| 18 19 20 21 22 23 24 | 16 17 18 19 20 21 22 | 20 21 22 23 24 25 26 | 18 19 20 21 22 23 24 |
| 25 26 27 28 29 30 | 23 24 25 26 27 28 29 | 27 28 29 30 | 25 26 27 28 29 30 31 |
| | 30 31 | | |

1

1. January has ___31___ days.

2. February has ___29___ days.

3. March has ___31___ days.

4. April has ___30___ days.

5. May has ___31___ days.

6. June has ___30___ days.

7. July has ___31___ days.

8. August has ___31___ days.

9. September has ___30___ days.

10. October has ___31___ days.

11. November has ___30___ days.

12. December has ___31___ days.

## Activity E: The Calendar  *page 34*

Listen to the sentences and look at them in your book.
Fill in the blanks with the correct number of days for
each month. Look at the calendar if you need help.   1

ACTIVITY F                    Name _____

# How Long Are the Months?

| January | February | March | April |
|---|---|---|---|
| S M T W T F S | S M T W T F S | S M T W T F S | S M T W T F S |
| 1 2 | 1 2 3 4 5 6 | 1 2 3 4 5 | 1 2 |
| 3 4 5 6 7 8 9 | 7 8 9 10 11 12 13 | 6 7 8 9 10 11 12 | 3 4 5 6 7 8 9 |
| 10 11 12 13 14 15 16 | 14 15 16 17 18 19 20 | 13 14 15 16 17 18 19 | 10 11 12 13 14 15 16 |
| 17 18 19 20 21 22 23 | 21 22 23 24 25 26 27 | 20 21 22 23 24 25 26 | 17 18 19 20 21 22 23 |
| 24 25 26 27 28 29 30 | 28 29 | 27 28 29 30 31 | 24 25 26 27 28 29 30 |
| 31 | | | |

| May | June | July | August |
|---|---|---|---|
| S M T W T F S | S M T W T F S | S M T W T F S | S M T W T F S |
| 1 2 3 4 5 6 7 | 1 2 3 4 | 1 2 | 1 2 3 4 5 6 |
| 8 9 10 11 12 13 14 | 5 6 7 8 9 10 11 | 3 4 5 6 7 8 9 | 7 8 9 10 11 12 13 |
| 15 16 17 18 19 20 21 | 12 13 14 15 16 17 18 | 10 11 12 13 14 15 16 | 14 15 16 17 18 19 20 |
| 22 23 24 25 26 27 28 | 19 20 21 22 23 24 25 | 17 18 19 20 21 22 23 | 21 22 23 24 25 26 27 |
| 29 30 31 | 26 27 28 29 30 | 24 25 26 27 28 29 30 | 28 29 30 31 |
| | | 31 | |

| September | October | November | December |
|---|---|---|---|
| S M T W T F S | S M T W T F S | S M T W T F S | S M T W T F S |
| 1 2 3 | 1 | 1 2 3 4 5 | 1 2 3 |
| 4 5 6 7 8 9 10 | 2 3 4 5 6 7 8 | 6 7 8 9 10 11 12 | 4 5 6 7 8 9 10 |
| 11 12 13 14 15 16 17 | 9 10 11 12 13 14 15 | 13 14 15 16 17 18 19 | 11 12 13 14 15 16 17 |
| 18 19 20 21 22 23 24 | 16 17 18 19 20 21 22 | 20 21 22 23 24 25 26 | 18 19 20 21 22 23 24 |
| 25 26 27 28 29 30 | 23 24 25 26 27 28 29 | 27 28 29 30 | 25 26 27 28 29 30 31 |
| | 30 31 | | |

| 31 Days | 30 Days | 28 or 29 Days |
|---|---|---|
| January | April | February |
| March | June | |
| May | September | |
| July | November | |
| August | | |
| October | | |
| December | | |

## Activity F: How Long Are the Months?  page 35

Listen to the sentences. Write the name of each month in the correct column in your book.

January has 31 days.

March has 31 days.

May has 31 days.

July has 31 days.

August has 31 days.

October has 31 days.

December has 31 days.

April has 30 days.

June has 30 days.

September has 30 days.

November has 30 days.

February has 28 or 29 days.

ACTIVITY G          Name _____

# Days and Dates

| January | February | March | April |
|---|---|---|---|
| S  M  T  W  T  F  S | S  M  T  W  T  F  S | S  M  T  W  T  F  S | S  M  T  W  T  F  S |
|            1  2 | 1  2  3  4  5  6 | 1  2  3  4  5 | 1  2 |
| 3  4  5  6  7  8  9 | 7  8  9 10 11 12 13 | 6  7  8  9 10 11 12 | 3  4  5  6  7  8  9 |
| 10 11 12 13 14 15 16 | 14 15 16 17 18 19 20 | 13 14 15 16 17 18 19 | 10 11 12 13 14 15 16 |
| 17 18 19 20 21 22 23 | 21 22 23 24 25 26 27 | 20 21 22 23 24 25 26 | 17 18 19 20 21 22 23 |
| 24 25 26 27 28 29 30 | 28 29 | 27 28 29 30 31 | 24 25 26 27 28 29 30 |
| 31 | | | |

| May | June | July | August |
|---|---|---|---|
| S  M  T  W  T  F  S | S  M  T  W  T  F  S | S  M  T  W  T  F  S | S  M  T  W  T  F  S |
| 1  2  3  4  5  6  7 | 1  2  3  4 | 1  2 | 1  2  3  4  5  6 |
| 8  9 10 11 12 13 14 | 5  6  7  8  9 10 11 | 3  4  5  6  7  8  9 | 7  8  9 10 11 12 13 |
| 15 16 17 18 19 20 21 | 12 13 14 15 16 17 18 | 10 11 12 13 14 15 16 | 14 15 16 17 18 19 20 |
| 22 23 24 25 26 27 28 | 19 20 21 22 23 24 25 | 17 18 19 20 21 22 23 | 21 22 23 24 25 26 27 |
| 29 30 31 | 26 27 28 29 30 | 24 25 26 27 28 29 30 | 28 29 30 31 |
| | | 31 | |

| September | October | November | December |
|---|---|---|---|
| S  M  T  W  T  F  S | S  M  T  W  T  F  S | S  M  T  W  T  F  S | S  M  T  W  T  F  S |
| 1  2  3 | 1 | 1  2  3  4  5 | 1  2  3 |
| 4  5  6  7  8  9 10 | 2  3  4  5  6  7  8 | 6  7  8  9 10 11 12 | 4  5  6  7  8  9 10 |
| 11 12 13 14 15 16 17 | 9 10 11 12 13 14 15 | 13 14 15 16 17 18 19 | 11 12 13 14 15 16 17 |
| 18 19 20 21 22 23 24 | 16 17 18 19 20 21 22 | 20 21 22 23 24 25 26 | 18 19 20 21 22 23 24 |
| 25 26 27 28 29 30 | 23 24 25 26 27 28 29 | 27 28 29 30 | 25 26 27 28 29 30 31 |
| | 30 31 | | |

**Sunday     Monday     Tuesday     Wednesday     Thursday     Friday     Saturday**

| | | | |
|---|---|---|---|
| January 20 | Wednesday | March 2 | Wednesday |
| February 15 | Monday | November 6 | Sunday |
| August 1 | Monday | May 30 | Monday |
| July 4 | Monday | October 31 | Monday |
| December 25 | Sunday | April 10 | Sunday |

## Activity G:  Days and Dates   *page 36*

Listen to the sentences. Write the correct day next to
each date. Look at the calendar if you need help.

January 20 is a Wednesday.

February 15 is a Monday.

August 1 is a Monday.

July 4 is a Monday.

December 25 is a Sunday.

March 2 is a Wednesday.

November 6 is a Sunday.

May 30 is a Monday.

October 31 is a Monday.

April 10 is a Sunday.

## ACTIVITY H

Name _____

## Dana's Calendar of Events

### MARCH

| S | M | T | W | T | F | S |
|---|---|---|---|---|---|---|
|  |  | 1 | 2 | 3 | 4 | 5<br>① 2:30<br>fishing |
| 6<br>② 6:00<br>tennis | 7 | 8 | 9 | 10 | 11 | 12 |
| 13<br>③ 4:15<br>swimming | 14 | 15 | 16 | 17 | 18 | 19<br>④ 3:15<br>baseball |
| 20 | 21<br>⑤ 12:45<br>lunch with<br>Yasuko | 22 | 23 | 24 | 25<br>⑥ 9:30<br>sailing | 26<br>⑦ 12:45<br>dentist's<br>appointment |
| 27 | 28 | 29 | 30 | 31<br>⑧ 11:15<br>doctor's<br>appointment |  |  |

| | Activity | Date | Time |
|---|---|---|---|
| 1. | fishing | March 5 | 2:30 |
| 2. | tennis | March 6 | 6:00 |
| 3. | swimming | March 13 | 4:15 |
| 4. | baseball | March 19 | 3:15 |
| 5. | lunch with Yasuko | March 21 | 12:45 |
| 6. | sailing | March 25 | 9:30 |
| 7. | dentist's appointment | March 26 | 12:45 |
| 8. | doctor's appointment | March 31 | 11:15 |

## Activity H: Dana's Calendar of Events *page 37*

Listen to the sentences and look at the calendar in your book. Write each activity, date, and time on the lines in your book.

1. Dana is going fishing on March 5 at 2:30.
2. She is playing tennis on March 6 at 6:00.
3. She is going swimming at 4:15 on March 13.
4. She has a baseball game at 3:15 on March 19.
5. She will have lunch with Yasuko on March 21 at 12:45.
6. She is going sailing at 9:30 on March 25.
7. Her dentist's appointment is at 12:45 on March 26.
8. She has a doctor's appointment on March 31 at 11:15.

---

### ACTIVITY I

Name _____

# Richard's Calendar of Events

## M A Y

| S | M | T | W | T | F | S |
|---|---|---|---|---|---|---|
| **1** | **2** | **3**<br>② 8:00<br>fishing | **4** | **5** | **6** | **7** |
| **8** | **9** | **10** | **11** | **12**<br>③ 12:00<br>tennis | **13** | **14**<br>④ 5:15<br>doctor's<br>appointment |
| **15**<br>⑤ 10:30<br>swimming | **16** | **17** | **18** | **19** | **20** | **21**<br>⑥ 1:00<br>baseball |
| **22**<br>⑦ 11:30<br>lunch with<br>Steve | **23** | **24** | **25** | **26** | **27** | **28**<br>⑧ 8:15<br>dentist's<br>appointment |
| **29**<br>① 1:00<br>sailing | **30** | **31** | | | | |

|   | Activity | Date | Time |
|---|---|---|---|
| 1. | sailing | May 29 | 1:00 |
| 2. | fishing | May 3 | 8:00 |
| 3. | tennis | May 12 | 12:00 |
| 4. | doctor's appointment | May 14 | 5:15 |
| 5. | swimming | May 15 | 10:30 |
| 6. | baseball | May 21 | 1:00 |
| 7. | lunch with Steve | May 22 | 11:30 |
| 8. | dentist's appointment | May 28 | 8:15 |

38    Learning to Listen in English

---

## Activity I:  Richard's Calendar of Events  *page 38*

Listen to the sentences. Write the activities and times on the correct dates on the calendar. Then write each activity, date, and time on the lines in your book.

1. Richard is going sailing on May 29 at 1:00.
2. On May 3 at 8:00 he is going fishing.
3. He is playing tennis on May 12 at 12:00.
4. He has a doctor's appointment on May 14 at 5:15.
5. He is going swimming on May 15 at 10:30.
6. He has a baseball game at 1:00 on May 21.
7. He is having lunch with Steve at 11:30 on May 22.
8. His dentist's appointment is at 8:15 on May 28.

ACTIVITY J

Name _____

# Steve's Calendar of Events

## A U G U S T

| S | M | T | W | T | F | S |
|---|---|---|---|---|---|---|
|  | 1<br>2:00<br>sailing | 2 | 3 | 4 | 5 | 6<br>3:15<br>baseball |
| 7 | 8 | 9<br>4:45<br>dentist's<br>appointment | 10 | 11 | 12 | 13 |
| 14 | 15 | 16 | 17 | 18 | 19 | 20 |
| 21 | 22 | 23 | 24<br>2:30<br>tennis | 25 | 26<br>12:20<br>lunch with<br>Richard | 27<br>8:00<br>baseball |
| 28<br>9:00<br>swimming | 29<br>9:00<br>swimming | 30<br>9:00<br>swimming | 31<br>7:00<br>fishing |  |  |  |

| | Activity | Date | Time |
|---|---|---|---|
| 1. | sailing | August 1 | 2:00 |
| 2. | baseball | August 6 | 3:15 |
| 3. | dentist's appointment | August 9 | 4:45 |
| 4. | tennis | August 24 | 2:30 |
| 5. | lunch with Richard | August 26 | 12:20 |
| 6. | baseball | August 27 | 8:00 |
| 7. | swimming | August 28, 29, 30 | 9:00 |
| 8. | fishing | August 31 | 7:00 |

Unit 3: Calendar Time    39

## Activity J: Steve's Calendar of Events  *page 39*

Listen to the sentences. Write the activities and times on the correct dates on the calendar. Then write each activity, date, and time on the lines in your book.

1. Steve is going sailing on August 1 at 2:00.
2. He is playing baseball at 3:15 on August 6.
3. His dentist's appointment is on August 9 at 4:45.
4. He is playing tennis at 2:30 on August 24.
5. He is going to meet Richard for lunch at 12:20 on August 26.
6. He will play baseball again at 8:00 on August 27.
7. He is going swimming at 9:00 on August 28, 29, and 30.
8. He will go fishing at 7:00 on August 31.

ACTIVITY K     Name _____

## Yasuko's Calendar of Events

### J U L Y

| S | M | T | W | T | F | S |
|---|---|---|---|---|---|---|
| | | | | | 1 | 2<br>6:15<br>fishing |
| 3  2:30<br>tennis | 4 | 5 | 6 | 7 | 8 | 9 |
| 10 | 11 | 12 | 13  12:45<br>doctor's<br>appointment | 14 | 15  1:00<br>lunch with<br>Dana | 16  5:00<br>tennis |
| 17  5:00<br>tennis | 18  5:00<br>tennis | 19  5:00<br>tennis | 20 | 21 | 22 | 23  7:00<br>baseball |
| 24  11:30<br>baseball | 25  7:20<br>dentist's<br>appointment | 26 | 27 | 28 | 29 | 30  8:30<br>sailing |
| 31  8:30<br>sailing | | | | | | |

| | Activity | Date | Time |
|---|---|---|---|
| 1. | fishing | July 2 | 6:15 |
| 2. | tennis | July 3 | 2:30 |
| 3. | doctor's appointment | July 13 | 12:45 |
| 4. | lunch with Dana | July 15 | 1:00 |
| 5. | tennis | July 16, 17, 18, 19 | 5:00 |
| 6. | baseball | July 23 | 7:00 |
| | | July 24 | 11:30 |
| 7. | dentist's appointment | July 25 | 7:20 |
| 8. | sailing | July 30, 31 | 8:30 |

## Activity K: Yasuko's Calendar of Events *page 40*

Listen to the sentences. Write the activities and times on the correct dates on the calendar. Then write each activity, date, and time on the lines in your book.

1. Yasuko is going fishing at 6:15 on July 2.
2. She is playing tennis at 2:30 on July 3.
3. Her doctor's appointment is at 12:45 on July 13.
4. She plans on meeting Dana for lunch at 1:00 on July 15.
5. On July 16, 17, 18, and 19 she is playing tennis at 5:00.
6. She has a baseball game on July 23 at 7:00, and on July 24 at 11:30.
7. Her dentist's appointment is on July 25 at 7:20.
8. She is going sailing on July 30 and 31 at 8:30.

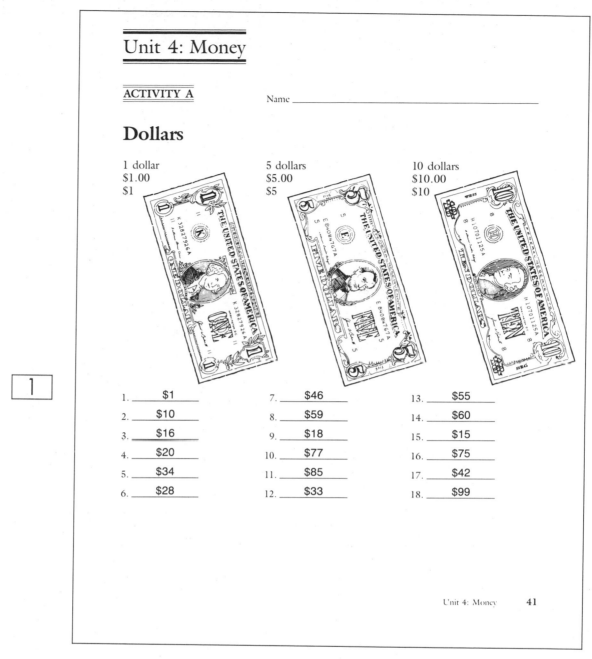

## Unit 4: Money

### Activity A: Dollars  *page 41*

Listen to these amounts of money. Look at the words, symbols, and pictures in your book.

   one dollar, one dollar, one dollar

   five dollars, five dollars, five dollars

   ten dollars, ten dollars, ten dollars

Now listen to these amounts of money and write them in your book. Use a dollar sign and numbers to write each amount.

Name _____

# Cents

| a quarter | a dime | a nickel | a penny |
|-----------|--------|----------|---------|
| 25 cents | 10 cents | 5 cents | 1 cent |
| 25¢ | 10¢ | 5¢ | 1¢ |
| $.25 | $.10 | $.05 | $.01 |

1

| 1. $.25 | 11. $.45 | 21. $.40 |
|---------|----------|----------|
| 2. $.10 | 12. $.17 | 22. $.19 |
| 3. $.45 | 13. $.64 | 23. $.40 |
| 4. $.77 | 14. $.22 | 24. $.88 |
| 5. $.56 | 15. $.35 | 25. $.68 |
| 6. $.88 | 16. $.73 | 26. $.36 |
| 7. $.91 | 17. $.29 | 27. $.72 |
| 8. $.65 | 18. $.80 | 28. $.15 |
| 9. $.16 | 19. $.60 | 29. $.11 |
| 10. $.90 | 20. $.90 | 30. $.20 |

## Activity B: Cents  *page 42*

Listen to these amounts of money. Look at the words, symbols, and pictures in your book.

a quarter, twenty-five cents, twenty-five cents, twenty-five cents

a dime, ten cents, ten cents, ten cents

a nickel, five cents, five cents, five cents

a penny, one cent, one cent, one cent

Now listen to these amounts of money and write them in your book. Use a dollar sign, decimal point, and numbers to write each amount.     1

Name _____

# Dollars and Cents

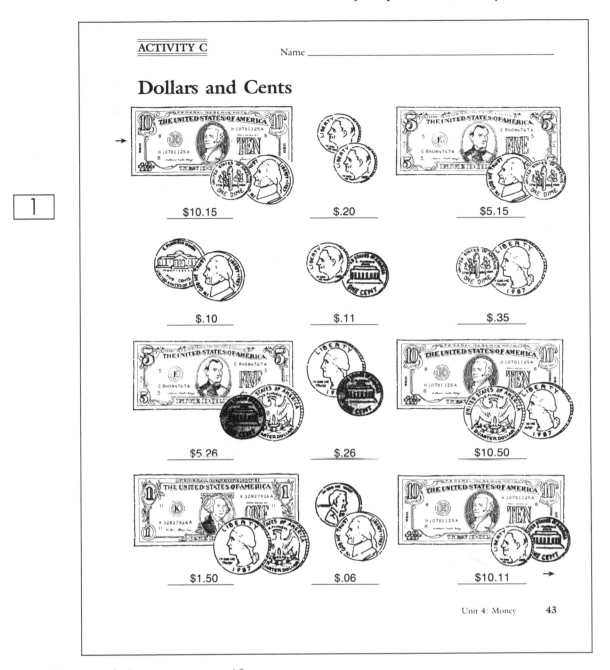

1

$10.15          $.20          $5.15

$.10          $.11          $.35

$5.26          $.26          $10.50

$1.50          $.06          $10.11

## Activity C:  Dollars and Cents  *pages 43 and 44*

Listen to these amounts of money and look at the pictures in your book. Write each amount on the line by the correct picture.

1

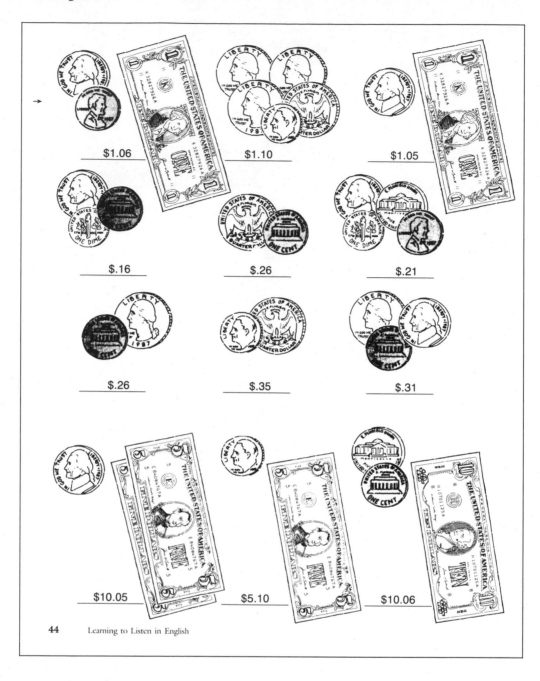

$1.06          $1.10          $1.05

$.16           $.26           $.21

$.26           $.35           $.31

$10.05         $5.10          $10.06

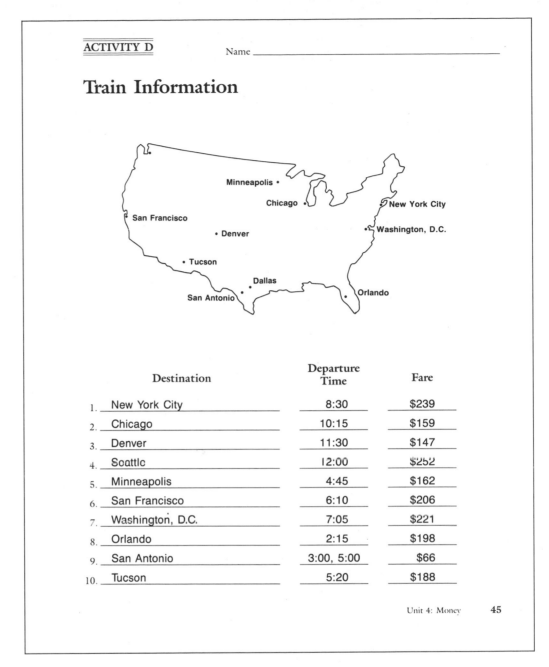

ACTIVITY D                Name _____

# Train Information

| Destination | Departure Time | Fare |
|---|---|---|
| 1. New York City | 8:30 | $239 |
| 2. Chicago | 10:15 | $159 |
| 3. Denver | 11:30 | $147 |
| 4. Seattle | 12:00 | $252 |
| 5. Minneapolis | 4:45 | $162 |
| 6. San Francisco | 6:10 | $206 |
| 7. Washington, D.C. | 7:05 | $221 |
| 8. Orlando | 2:15 | $198 |
| 9. San Antonio | 3:00, 5:00 | $66 |
| 10. Tucson | 5:20 | $188 |

Unit 4: Money    **45**

## Activity D: Train Information  *page 45*

Listen to the sentences. Write each destination, departure time, and fare on the lines in your book. Look at the map if you need help.

1. The train for New York City leaves at 8:30. The fare is $239.
2. The train for Chicago leaves at 10:15. The fare is $159.
3. The train for Denver leaves at 11:30. The fare is $147.
4. The train for Seattle leaves at 12:00. The fare is $252.
5. The train for Minneapolis leaves at 4:45. The fare is $162.
6. The train for San Francisco leaves at 6:10. The fare is $206.
7. The train for Washington, D.C. leaves at 7:05. The fare is $221.
8. The train for Orlando leaves at 2:15. The fare is $198.
9. There are trains for San Antonio at 3:00 and at 5:00. The fare is $66.
10. The train for Tucson leaves at 5:20. The fare is $188.

## Unit 5: The Planets

ACTIVITY A

Name _____

# The Planets

Sun    Mercury    Venus    Earth    Mars    Jupiter    Saturn    Uranus    Neptune    O Pluto

1

(Students will hear the name of each planet only one time.)

| | | |
|---|---|---|
| 1. Mercury | Mercury | |
| 2. Venus | Venus | |
| 3. Earth | Earth | |
| 4. Mars | Mars | |
| 5. Jupiter | Jupiter | |
| 6. Saturn | Saturn | |
| 7. Uranus | Uranus | |
| 8. Neptune | Neptune | |
| 9. Pluto | Pluto | |

## Unit 5: The Planets

### Activity A: The Planets  *page 46*

Listen to the names of the planets and look at the picture in your book.

Mercury, Venus, Earth, Mars, Jupiter, Saturn, Uranus, Neptune, Pluto

Now listen again and write the names of the planets on the lines in your book. 1

ACTIVITY B                    Name _____

# Bigger and Smaller

| PART 1 | | PART 2 | |
|---|---|---|---|
| **Smaller** | | **Bigger** | |
| 1. __Pluto__ | Mercury | 11. __Jupiter__ | Saturn |
| 2. __Mercury__ | Mars | 12. __Saturn__ | Uranus |
| 3. __Mars__ | Venus | 13. __Uranus__ | Neptune |
| 4. __Venus__ | Earth | 14. __Neptune__ | Earth |
| 5. __Earth__ | Neptune | 15. __Earth__ | Venus |
| 6. __Neptune__ | Uranus | 16. __Venus__ | Mars |
| 7. __Uranus__ | Saturn | 17. __Mars__ | Mercury |
| 8. __Earth__ | Saturn | 18. __Mercury__ | Pluto |
| 9. __Mercury__ | Jupiter | 19. __Jupiter__ | Pluto |
| 10. __Saturn__ | Jupiter | 20. __Jupiter__ | Mercury |

Unit 5: The Planets    47

## Activity B: *Bigger* and *Smaller*

**Part 1** *page 47*

Listen to the sentences. Write the planet that is *smaller* than each planet in your book.

1. Pluto is smaller than Mercury.
2. Mercury is smaller than Mars.
3. Mars is smaller than Venus.
4. Venus is smaller than Earth.
5. Earth is smaller than Neptune.
6. Neptune is smaller than Uranus.
7. Uranus is smaller than Saturn.
8. Earth is smaller than Saturn.
9. Mercury is smaller than Jupiter.
10. Saturn is smaller than Jupiter.

### *Bigger* and *Smaller*
**Part 2** *page 47*

Listen to the sentences. Write the planet that is *bigger* than each planet in your book.

11. Jupiter is bigger than Saturn.
12. Saturn is bigger than Uranus.
13. Uranus is bigger than Neptune.
14. Neptune is bigger than Earth.
15. Earth is bigger than Venus.
16. Venus is bigger than Mars.
17. Mars is bigger than Mercury.
18. Mercury is bigger than Pluto.
19. Jupiter is bigger than Pluto.
20. Jupiter is bigger than Mercury.

Name _____

# Sentences with Bigger and Smaller

1. _____Pluto_____ is smaller than Mercury.
2. _____Mercury_____ is smaller than Mars.
3. _____Mars_____ is smaller than _____Venus_____.
4. _____Venus_____ is smaller than _____Earth_____.
5. _____Earth_____ is smaller than _____Neptune_____.
6. _____Neptune_____ is smaller than _____Uranus_____.
7. _____Uranus_____ is smaller than _____Saturn_____.
8. _____Earth_____ is smaller than _____Saturn_____.
9. _____Mercury_____ is _____smaller_____ than _____Jupiter_____.
10. _____Saturn_____ is _____smaller_____ than _____Jupiter_____.
11. _____Pluto_____ is _____smaller_____ than _____Neptune_____.
12. _____Mercury_____ is _____smaller_____ than _____Earth_____.
13. _____Jupiter_____ is bigger than Saturn.
14. _____Saturn_____ is bigger than Uranus.
15. _____Uranus_____ is bigger than Neptune.
16. _____Neptune_____ is bigger than _____Earth_____.
17. _____Earth_____ is bigger than _____Venus_____.
18. _____Venus_____ is bigger than _____Mars_____.
19. _____Mars_____ is bigger than _____Mercury_____.
20. _____Mercury_____ is bigger than _____Pluto_____.
21. _____Jupiter_____ is bigger than _____Pluto_____.
22. _____Jupiter_____ is _____bigger_____ than _____Mercury_____.
23. _____Earth_____ is _____bigger_____ than _____Mars_____.
24. _____Earth_____ is _____bigger_____ than _____Mercury_____.

## Activity C:  Sentences with *Bigger* and *Smaller*   *page 48*

Listen to the sentences. Write the missing words in your book.

1

ACTIVITY D          Name _____

# Closer to and Farther from

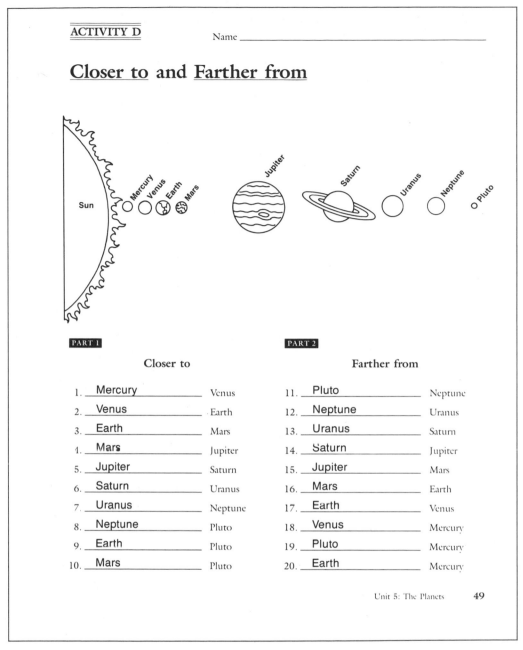

PART 1

**Closer to**

1. __Mercury_____ Venus
2. __Venus_____ Earth
3. __Earth_____ Mars
4. __Mars_____ Jupiter
5. __Jupiter_____ Saturn
6. __Saturn_____ Uranus
7. __Uranus_____ Neptune
8. __Neptune_____ Pluto
9. __Earth_____ Pluto
10. __Mars_____ Pluto

PART 2

**Farther from**

11. __Pluto_____ Neptune
12. __Neptune_____ Uranus
13. __Uranus_____ Saturn
14. __Saturn_____ Jupiter
15. __Jupiter_____ Mars
16. __Mars_____ Earth
17. __Earth_____ Venus
18. __Venus_____ Mercury
19. __Pluto_____ Mercury
20. __Earth_____ Mercury

Unit 5: The Planets    **49**

## Activity D: *Closer to* and *Farther from*

**Part 1**  *page 49*

Listen to the sentences. Write the planet that is closer to the sun in your book.

1. Mercury is closer to the sun than Venus.
2. Venus is closer to the sun than Earth.
3. Earth is closer to the sun than Mars.
4. Mars is closer to the sun than Jupiter.
5. Jupiter is closer to the sun than Saturn.
6. Saturn is closer to the sun than Uranus.
7. Uranus is closer to the sun than Neptune.
8. Neptune is closer to the sun than Pluto.
9. Earth is closer to the sun than Pluto.
10. Mars is closer to the sun than Pluto.

*Closer to* and *Farther from*

**Part 2**  *page 49*

Listen to the sentences. Write the planet that is farther from the sun in your book.

11. Pluto is farther from the sun than Neptune.
12. Neptune is farther from the sun than Uranus.
13. Uranus is farther from the sun than Saturn.
14. Saturn is farther from the sun than Jupiter.
15. Jupiter is farther from the sun than Mars.
16. Mars is farther from the sun than Earth.
17. Earth is farther from the sun than Venus.
18. Venus is farther from the sun than Mercury.
19. Pluto is farther from the sun than Mercury.
20. Earth is farther from the sun than Mercury.

---

ACTIVITY E

Name _____

# Sentences with <u>Closer to</u> and <u>Farther from</u>

1. _____Mercury_____ is closer to the sun than Venus.
2. _____Venus_____ is closer to the sun than Earth.
3. _____Earth_____ is closer to the sun than Mars.
4. _____Mars_____ is closer to the sun than Jupiter.
5. _____Jupiter_____ is closer to the sun than _____Saturn_____.
6. _____Saturn_____ is closer to the sun than _____Uranus_____.
7. _____Uranus_____ is closer to the sun than _____Neptune_____.
8. _____Neptune_____ is _____closer_____ _to_ the sun than _____Pluto_____.
9. _____Earth_____ is _____closer_____ _to_ the sun than _____Pluto_____.
10. _____Mars_____ is _____closer_____ _to_ the sun than _____Pluto_____.
11. _____Pluto_____ is farther from the sun than Neptune.
12. _____Neptune_____ is farther from the sun than Uranus.
13. _____Uranus_____ is farther from the sun than Saturn.
14. _____Saturn_____ is farther from the sun than Jupiter.
15. _____Jupiter_____ is farther from the sun than _____Mars_____.
16. _____Mars_____ is farther from the sun than _____Earth_____.
17. _____Earth_____ is farther from the sun than _____Venus_____.
18. _____Venus_____ is _____farther_____ _from_ the sun than _____Mercury_____.
19. _____Pluto_____ is _____farther_____ _from_ the sun than _____Mercury_____.
20. _____Earth_____ is _____farther_____ _from_ the sun than _____Mercury_____.

---

## Activity E: Sentences with *Closer to* and *Farther from* page 50

Listen to the sentences. Write the missing words in your book.

### ACTIVITY F

Name _____

# Numbers
**PART 1**

**1**

→ 100  __110__  __135__  __144__  __156__  __188__  __190__  __191__
200  __244__  __250__  300  __375__  __378__  400  __415__
500  __515__  600  __666__  700  __789__  800  __801__
900  __910__

**2**

| | | | | | |
|---|---|---|---|---|---|
| 1. __927__ | 16. __754__ | 31. __657__ |
| 2. __654__ | 17. __308__ | 32. __748__ |
| 3. __490__ | 18. __200__ | 33. __920__ |
| 4. __876__ | 19. __911__ | 34. __823__ |
| 5. __901__ | 20. __421__ | 35. __717__ |
| 6. __777__ | 21. __320__ | 36. __101__ |
| 7. __854__ | 22. __403__ | 37. __830__ |
| 8. __345__ | 23. __566__ | 38. __539__ |
| 9. __600__ | 24. __855__ | 39. __859__ |
| 10. __432__ | 25. __300__ | 40. __927__ |
| 11. __743__ | 26. __770__ | 41. __537__ |
| 12. __701__ | 27. __903__ | 42. __435__ |
| 13. __541__ | 28. __605__ | 43. __320__ |
| 14. __807__ | 29. __913__ | 44. __119__ |
| 15. __400__ | 30. __743__ | 45. __204__ |

## Activity F: Numbers

**Part 1**  *page 51*
Listen to these rows of numbers. Write the missing numbers in your book.  **1**

Now listen to these numbers and write them in your book.  **2**

PART 2                                     Name _____

### 1

→  1,000    __2,000__    3,000    __4,000__    5,000    __5,500__
   6,000    __6,500__    7,000    __7,500__    8,000    __8,500__
   9,000    __9,500__    10,000   __11,000__   12,000   __12,500__
   13,000   __14,000__   15,000
   20,000   __30,000__   40,000   __50,000__   60,000   __70,000__
   80,000   __90,000__

### 2

| | | | | |
|---|---|---|---|---|
| 1. | __1,234__ | | 16. | __6,984__ |
| 2. | __2,300__ | | 17. | __9,784__ |
| 3. | __6,500__ | | 18. | __6,784__ |
| 4. | __4,415__ | | 19. | __5,005__ |
| 5. | __1,200__ | | 20. | __8,432__ |
| 6. | __7,000__ | | 21. | __8,989__ |
| 7. | __2,413__ | | 22. | __1,030__ |
| 8. | __5,430__ | | 23. | __2,022__ |
| 9. | __7,611__ | | 24. | __3,728__ |
| 10. | __6,002__ | | 25. | __4,539__ |
| 11. | __5,003__ | | 26. | __10,550__ |
| 12. | __4,300__ | | 27. | __60,970__ |
| 13. | __4,303__ | | 28. | __30,500__ |
| 14. | __8,765__ | | 29. | __45,500__ |
| 15. | __7,895__ | | 30. | __88,850__ |

## Numbers

**Part 2**  *page 52*

Listen to these rows of numbers. Write the missing numbers in your book. [1]

Now listen to these numbers and write them in your book. [2]

PART 3                     Name _____

**1**

→      100,000 ___200,000___  300,000 ___400,000___  500,000 ___600,000___

       700,000 ___800,000___  900,000

       1,000,000 ___2,000,000___  3,000,000 ___4,000,000___

       5,000,000 ___6,000,000___  7,000,000 ___8,000,000___

       9,000,000 ___10,000,000___  11,000,000 ___12,000,000___

       20,000,000 ___30,000,000___  40,000,000 ___50,000,000___

       60,000,000 ___70,000,000___  80,000,000 ___90,000,000___

       100,000,000 ___200,000,000___  300,000,000 ___400,000,000___

**2**

1. ___125,435___           11. ___7,500,450___
2. ___340,894___           12. ___2,900,456___
3. ___567,785___           13. ___5,550,200___
4. ___612,009___           14. ___6,400,389___
5. ___400,500___           15. ___8,880,820___
6. ___850,463___           16. ___20,900,950___
7. ___725,000___           17. ___35,900,950___
8. ___945,783___           18. ___44,800,000___
9. ___650,473___           19. ___35,530,000___
10. ___1,500,007___        20. ___62,400,000___

## Numbers
**Part 3**  *page 53*

Listen to these rows of numbers. Write the missing numbers in your book.  **1**

Now listen to these numbers and write them in your book.  **2**

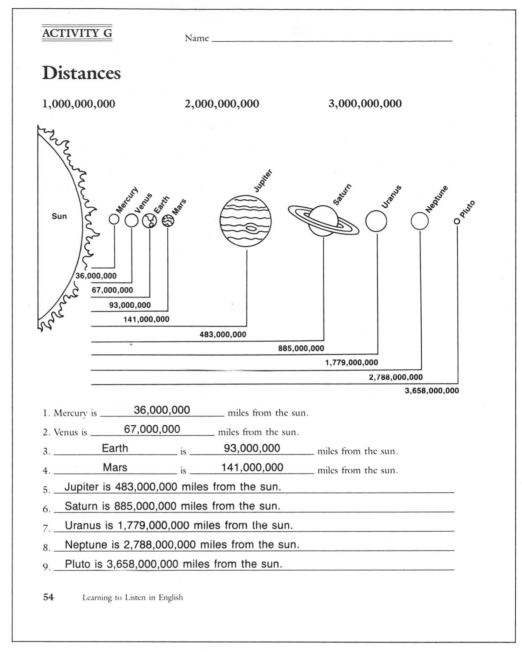

Name _____

# Distances

1,000,000,000        2,000,000,000        3,000,000,000

Sun    Mercury  Venus  Earth  Mars        Jupiter        Saturn        Uranus        Neptune        Pluto

36,000,000
67,000,000
93,000,000
141,000,000
483,000,000
885,000,000
1,779,000,000
2,788,000,000
3,658,000,000

1. Mercury is _____36,000,000_____ miles from the sun.

2. Venus is _____67,000,000_____ miles from the sun.

3. _____Earth_____ is _____93,000,000_____ miles from the sun.

4. _____Mars_____ is _____141,000,000_____ miles from the sun.

5. _Jupiter is 483,000,000 miles from the sun._____

6. _Saturn is 885,000,000 miles from the sun._____

7. _Uranus is 1,779,000,000 miles from the sun._____

8. _Neptune is 2,788,000,000 miles from the sun._____

9. _Pluto is 3,658,000,000 miles from the sun._____

## Activity G: Distances  *page 54*

Listen to the sentences and write the missing words in your book. Look at the picture if you need help.

1. Mercury is 36 million miles from the sun.
2. Venus is 67 million miles from the sun.
3. Earth is 93 million miles from the sun.
4. Mars is 141 million miles from the sun.
5. Jupiter is 483 million miles from the sun.
6. Saturn is 885 million miles from the sun.
7. Uranus is 1 billion, 779 million miles from the sun.
8. Neptune is 2 billion, 788 million miles from the sun.
9. Pluto is 3 billion, 658 million miles from the sun.

## ACTIVITY H

Name _____

# Diameter

Pluto 1,860
Mercury 3,026
Mars 4,208
Venus 7,504
Earth 7,909
Neptune 30,690
Uranus 32,116
Saturn 74,400
Jupiter 88,536

1. The diameter of Mercury is _____3,026_____ miles.

2. The diameter of _____Venus_____ is _____7,504_____ miles.

3. The diameter of _____Earth_____ is _____7,909_____ miles.

4. ____The diameter of Mars is 4,208 miles._____

5. ____The diameter of Jupiter is 88,536 miles._____

6. ____The diameter of Saturn is 74,400 miles._____

7. ____The diameter of Uranus is 32,116 miles._____

8. ____The diameter of Neptune is 30,690 miles._____

9. ____The diameter of Pluto is 1,860 miles._____

## Activity H: Diameter  page 55

Listen to the sentences and write the missing words in your book. Look at the picture if you need help.  ☐ 1

**ACTIVITY I**

Name _____

# Order

Sun    Mercury    Venus    Earth    Mars    Jupiter    Saturn    Uranus    Neptune    O Pluto

| first | second | third | fourth | fifth | sixth | seventh | eighth | ninth |
| 1st | 2nd | 3rd | 4th | 5th | 6th | 7th | 8th | 9th |

□ 1

□ 2

□ 3

**PART 1**

1. Mercury is the _____first_____ planet from the sun.

2. Venus is the _____second_____ planet from the sun.

3. _____Earth_____ is the _____third_____ planet from the sun.

4. _____Mars_____ is the _____fourth_____ planet from the sun.

5. ___Jupiter is the fifth planet from the sun.___

6. ___Saturn is the sixth planet from the sun.___

7. ___Uranus is the seventh planet from the sun.___

8. ___Neptune is the eighth planet from the sun.___

9. ___Pluto is the ninth planet from the sun.___

**PART 2**

1. The _____first_____ planet is Mercury.

2. The _____second_____ planet is Venus.

3. The _____third_____ planet is _____Earth_____.

4. The _____fourth_____ planet is _____Mars_____.

5. ___The fifth planet is Jupiter.___

6. ___The sixth planet is Saturn.___

7. ___The seventh planet is Uranus.___

8. ___The eighth planet is Neptune.___

9. ___The ninth planet is Pluto.___

## Activity I: Order

**Part 1**  *page 56*

Listen to these ordinal numbers and look at them in your book.  □ 1

Now listen to the sentences and write the missing words in your book. Look at the picture if you need help.  □ 2

## Order

**Part 2**  *page 56*

Listen to the sentences and write the missing words in your book. Look at the picture if you need help.  □ 3

# Unit 6: Food

ACTIVITY A

Name _____

## Food

PART 1

1

corn

bread

muffin

celery

cheese

carrots

tomato

apple

eggs

ice cream

hamburger

hot dog

# Unit 6: Food

## Activity A: Foods

**Part 1**  *page 57*

Listen to the names of these foods. Look at the words and pictures in your book.    1

Name _____

1

| | | |
|---|---|---|
| corn | bread | muffin |
| celery | cheese | carrots |
| tomato | apple | eggs |
| ice cream | hamburger | hot dog |

**Foods**
**Part 2**  *page 58*
Listen and write the name of each food by its picture.    1

1

(Students will hear the name of each food only one time.)

ACTIVITY B                     Name _____

# Alphabetical Order

| | |
|---|---|
| apple | apple |
| bread | bread |
| carrots | carrots |
| celery | celery |
| cheese | cheese |
| corn | corn |
| eggs | eggs |
| hamburger | hamburger |
| hot dog | hot dog |
| ice cream | ice cream |
| muffin | muffin |
| tomato | tomato |

Unit 6: Food    59

## Activity B:  Alphabetical Order  *page 59*

Listen to the names of these foods. They are in alphabetical order. Write them on the lines in your book.

1

# Breakfast, Lunch, and Dinner
PART 1

| Breakfast | Lunch | Dinner |
|-----------|-------|--------|
| eggs | hot dog | hamburger |
| bread | carrots | muffin |
|  | celery | cheese |
|  | apple | corn |
|  |  | tomato |
|  |  | ice cream |

| Breakfast | Lunch | Dinner |
|-----------|-------|--------|
| eggs | hot dog | hamburger |
| bread | carrots | muffin |
|  | celery | cheese |
|  | apple | corn |
|  |  | tomato |
|  |  | ice cream |

## Activity C: Breakfast, Lunch, and Dinner

**Part 1**   *page 60*

Listen to the dialogue. Write the names of the foods in the correct columns. Look at the top of the page if you need help.

What do you have for breakfast?

Eggs and bread.

How about lunch?

A hot dog, carrots, celery, and an apple.

And for dinner?

For dinner I have a hamburger, a muffin, cheese, corn, a tomato, and ice cream.

**PART 2**                    Name _____

**Dana**

1. Dana has eggs and bread for breakfast.
2. She has a hamburger and a carrot for _____lunch_____.
3. For dinner, she has a tomato, celery, a _____hot dog_____, and _____cheese_____.

**Richard**

4. Richard has a _____muffin_____ and a tomato for _____breakfast_____.
5. He has a _____hot dog_____, corn, and cheese for _____lunch_____.
6. For _____dinner_____, he has a hamburger and _____carrots_____.

**Steve**

7. Steve has a hot dog for _____breakfast_____.
8. He _____has eggs and cheese for lunch_____.
9. For _____dinner, he has a hamburger and a tomato_____

**Yasuko**

10. Yasuko _____has bread and cheese for breakfast_____.
11. _____She has a hot dog and an apple for lunch._____
12. _____For dinner, she has a muffin, celery, eggs, and ice cream._____

Unit 6: Food    **61**

**Breakfast, Lunch, and Dinner**
**Part 2** *page 61*
Listen to the sentences. Write the missing words in your book.  [ 1 ]

<u>**ACTIVITY D**</u>    Name _____

# Menus

| | Dana | Richard | Steve | Yasuko |
|---|:---:|:---:|:---:|:---:|
| apples | ✔ | | ✔ | ✔ |
| bread | ✔ | | ✔ | ✔ |
| carrots | ✔ | ✔ | ✔ | |
| celery | | | ✔ | ✔ |
| cheese | ✔ | | | |
| eggs | | ✔ | | ✔ |
| hamburgers | | ✔ | ✔ | |
| hot dogs | ✔ | | | ✔ |
| ice cream | ✔ | ✔ | ✔ | ✔ |
| muffins | | ✔ | | |
| tomatoes | | | ✔ | ✔ |

## Activity D: Menus  *page 62*

Listen to the sentences and look at the list of foods in your book. Put a check mark in the box under the name of each person who likes that kind of food.

Dana, Steve, and Yasuko like apples.

Yasuko, Steve, and Dana like bread.

Dana, Richard, and Steve like carrots.

Steve and Yasuko like celery.

Dana likes cheese.

Richard and Yasuko like eggs.

Richard and Steve like hamburgers.

Dana and Yasuko like hot dogs.

Dana, Richard, Steve, and Yasuko like ice cream.

Richard likes muffins.

Steve and Yasuko like tomatoes.

ACTIVITY E                Name _____

# More Foods
**PART 1**

coffee          fish          bananas          pear

potato          tortillas          orange          beans

milk          strawberries          rice          squash

Unit 6: Food    63

## Activity E: More Foods

**Part 1**  *page 63*
Listen to the names of these foods. Look at the words
and pictures in your book.  1

**More Foods**
**Part 2**  *page 64*
Listen and write the name of each food by its picture.    1

ACTIVITY F

ACTIVITY F                    Name _____

# At the Supermarket

| | |
|---|---|
| apples | $ .29 |
| bananas | $ .33 |
| beans | $ .79 |
| bread | $1.25 |
| carrots | $ .88 |
| celery | $ .89 |
| cheese | $2.04 |
| coffee | $3.49 |
| corn | $ .18 |
| eggs | $1.50 |
| fish | $3.75 |
| hamburgers | $2.88 |
| hot dogs | $1.88 |
| ice cream | $3.99 |
| milk | $2.09 |
| muffins | $ .25 |
| oranges | $2.35 |
| pears | $2.86 |
| potatoes | $2.55 |
| rice | $1.45 |
| squash | $ .88 |
| strawberries | $1.11 |
| tomatoes | $ .99 |
| tortillas | $1.69 |

## Activity F:  At the Supermarket   *page 65*

Listen to the sentences. Write the correct price next to the name of each food in your book.

Apples cost 29 cents. Bananas are 33 cents; and beans, 79 cents. Bread is $1.25; carrots, 88 cents; celery, 89 cents; and cheese, $2.04. Coffee is $3.49; corn, 18 cents; eggs, $1.50; fish, $3.75, and hamburgers, $2.88.

Hot dogs are $1.88; ice cream, $3.99; milk, $2.09; muffins, 25 cents; oranges, $2.35; pears, $2.86; and potatoes, $2.55.
Rice is $1.45, squash, 88 cents; strawberries, $1.11; tomatoes, 99 cents; and tortillas, $1.69.

<u>ACTIVITY G</u>    Name _____

# Breakfast Menu for the Week

| Sunday | Monday | Tuesday |
|---|---|---|
| milk | eggs | apple |
| bread | muffins | cheese |
| coffee | strawberries | coffee |

| Wednesday | Thursday | Friday |
|---|---|---|
| rice | eggs | muffins |
| beans | cheese | strawberries |
| milk | tomato | milk |

| Saturday |
|---|
| beans |
| tortillas |
| strawberries |

## Activity G: Breakfast Menu for the Week  *page 66*

Listen to the dialogue. Write the names of the foods under the correct days in your book.

What will we have on Sunday?

Sunday? Milk, bread, and coffee. How about Monday?

Let's have eggs, muffins, and strawberries. Tuesday?

An apple, cheese, and coffee. Wednesday?

Wednesday? How about rice, beans, and milk? Thursday?

Eggs, cheese, and a tomato. Friday?

Let's have muffins, strawberries, and milk. What about Saturday?

Beans, tortillas, and strawberries.

ACTIVITY H

Name _____

# Lunch Menu for the Week

| Sunday | Monday | Tuesday |
|---|---|---|
| fish | hot dogs | hamburgers |
| rice | cheese | carrots |
| tortillas | tomatoes | oranges |
| bananas | milk | bread |

| Wednesday | Thursday | Friday |
|---|---|---|
| eggs | fish | rice |
| cheese | potatoes | beans |
| tortillas | strawberries | tortillas |
| beans | ice cream | pears |

### Saturday

cheese

muffins

corn

apples

Unit 6: Food    67

## Activity H: Lunch Menu for the Week  *page 67*

Listen to the dialogue. Write the names of the foods under the correct days in your book.

What shall we have for lunch on Sunday?

Fish, rice, tortillas, and bananas. Monday?

Hot dogs, cheese, tomatoes, and milk. Tuesday?

Hamburgers, carrots, oranges, and bread. Wednesday?

Eggs, cheese, tortillas, and beans. Thursday?

Fish again, with potatoes, strawberries, and ice cream. Friday?

On Friday, let's have rice, beans, tortillas, and pears. Saturday?

Cheese, muffins, corn, and apples.

# Dinner Menu for the Week

| Sunday | Monday | Tuesday |
|--------|--------|---------|
| corn | rice | eggs |
| carrots | fish | beans |
| eggs | celery | pears |
| milk | ice cream | coffee |

| Wednesday | Thursday | Friday |
|-----------|----------|--------|
| squash | fish | muffins |
| tomatoes | beans | potatoes |
| rice | rice | cheese |
| beans | bananas | ice cream |

**Saturday**

hamburgers
tomatoes
milk
strawberries

## Activity I: Dinner Menu for the Week  *page 68*

Listen to the dialogue. Write the names of the foods under the correct days in your book.

On Sunday, let's have corn, carrots, eggs, and milk.

Okay. And let's have rice, fish, celery, and ice cream on Monday.

Sounds good. How about eggs, beans, pears, and coffee on Tuesday?

Sure. What about squash, tomatoes, rice, and beans on Wednesday?

Fine. I would like to try fish again, with beans, rice, and bananas on Thursday.

Great. Let's have muffins, potatoes, cheese, and ice cream on Friday.

All right. And I'd like hamburgers, tomatoes, milk, and strawberries on Saturday.

Name _____

# Restaurant Menu

**Breakfast**

| | | |
|---|---|---|
| 2 eggs and a muffin, bread, or tortillas | | $3.25 |
| Juice | | |
| Apple, tomato, orange | small | $ .65 |
| | medium | $1.10 |
| | large | $1.65 |
| Milk, coffee | small | $ .55 |
| | large | $1.00 |

**Lunch**

| | |
|---|---|
| Hamburger, cheese, and tomato | $2.85 |
| Hot dog, beans | $2.45 |

**Dinner**

| | |
|---|---|
| Fish, rice, beans, tortillas | $8.95 |
| Hamburger, potatoes, squash, corn | $7.95 |
| Hot dog, tomato, celery | $6.95 |
| Eggs, cheese, beans, rice | $5.95 |

**Dessert**

| | |
|---|---|
| Ice cream | $1.65 |
| Apples and cheese | $2.50 |
| Strawberries | $1.85 |
| Pears | $1.35 |

## Activity J: Restaurant Menu  *page 69*

Listen to the dialogue. Write the price of each item on the menu in your book.

What is on the menu?

Well, for breakfast they have two eggs and a muffin, bread, or tortillas for $3.25.

What about to drink?

Apple, tomato, or orange juice: small, 65 cents; medium, $1.10; or large, $1.65. Or you can have milk or coffee: small, 55 cents, and large, $1.00.

How about lunch?

You can have a hamburger, cheese, and tomato for $2.85, or a hot dog with beans for $2.45.

And dinner, what about dinner?

Fish with rice, beans, and tortillas, $8.95; hamburger with potatoes, squash, and corn, $7.95; a hot dog with tomato and celery, $6.95; or eggs with cheese, beans, and rice, $5.95.

What about dessert?

There is ice cream, $1.65; apples and cheese, $2.50; strawberries, $1.85; and pears, $1.35.

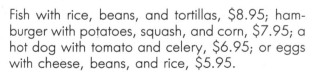

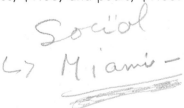

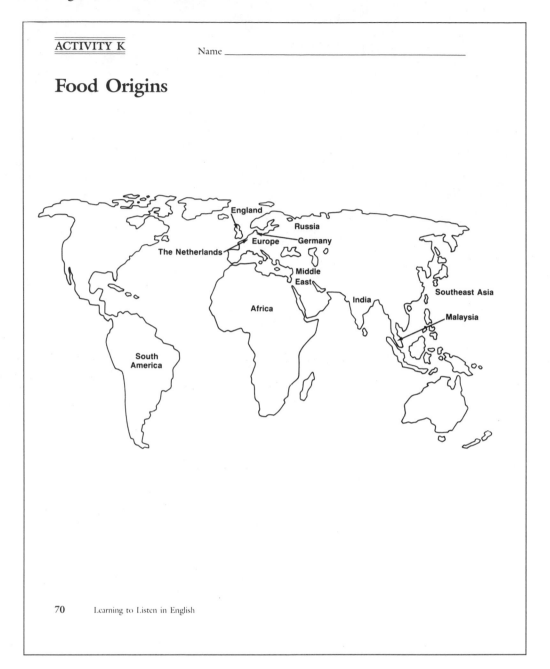

ACTIVITY K                    Name _____

# Food Origins

South America

Africa

England

Russia

Europe   Germany

The Netherlands

Middle East

India

Southeast Asia

Malaysia

## Activity K: Food Origins   *pages 70 and 71*

Listen to the dialogue and look at the map in your book.

Did you know that apples are from Russia?

Really? Bananas are from Malaysia; that I knew.

And beans are from Africa.

Carrots come from the Middle East, and eggs are from India.

Hot dogs and hamburgers are from Germany.

Milk and cheese come from The Netherlands, and oranges are from Southeast Asia.

Pears are from Europe, and potatoes are from Europe, too.

What about rice?

Rice is from Southeast Asia.

And squash, where's that from?

Squash is from South America.

Name _____

| | |
|---|---|
| apples | Russia |
| bananas | Malaysia |
| beans | Africa |
| carrots | Middle East |
| eggs | India |
| hamburgers | Germany |
| hot dogs | Germany |
| milk, cheese | The Netherlands |
| oranges | Southeast Asia |
| pears | Europe |
| potatoes | Europe |
| rice | Southeast Asia |
| squash | South America |

Unit 6: Food    71

Now listen to these sentences. Write the names of the missing foods and countries in your book.

Apples are from Russia.

Bananas are from Malaysia.

Beans are from Africa.

Carrots are from the Middle East.

Eggs are from India.

Hamburgers are from Germany.

Hot dogs are from Germany.

Milk and cheese are from The Netherlands.

Oranges are from Southeast Asia.

Pears are from Europe.

Potatoes are from Europe.

Rice is from Southeast Asia.

Squash is from South America.

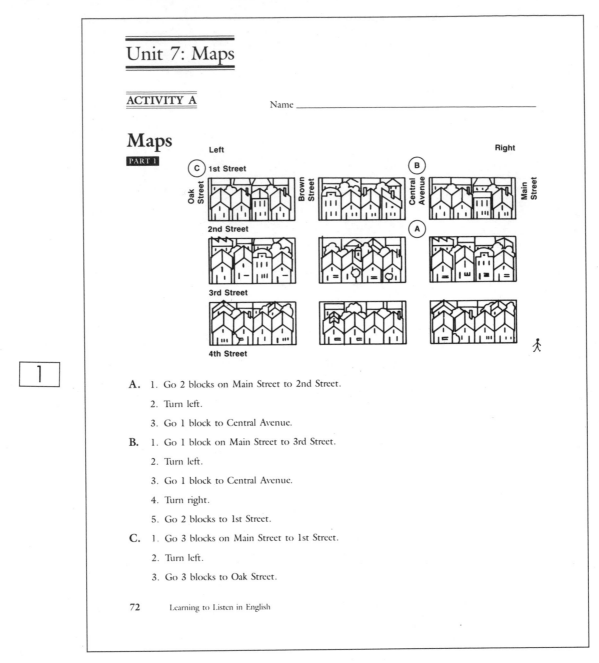

## Unit 7: Maps

ACTIVITY A    Name _____

**Maps**
PART 1

**A.**  1. Go 2 blocks on Main Street to 2nd Street.

2. Turn left.

3. Go 1 block to Central Avenue.

**B.**  1. Go 1 block on Main Street to 3rd Street.

2. Turn left.

3. Go 1 block to Central Avenue.

4. Turn right.

5. Go 2 blocks to 1st Street.

**C.**  1. Go 3 blocks on Main Street to 1st Street.

2. Turn left.

3. Go 3 blocks to Oak Street.

72    Learning to Listen in English

## Unit 7: Maps

### Activity A: Maps

**Part 1**  *page 72*
Listen to the directions and look at the map in your book. For each set of directions, start with your finger on the little person in the lower right corner of the map. Use your finger to follow the directions on the map. At the end of each set of directions, you should find the correct letter written on the map. ⎡1⎤

PART 2                                    Name _____

A.  Go on 4th Street to Central Avenue.

B.  Go on 4th Street to Brown Street.

C.  1. Go on Main Street to 3rd Street.

    2. Turn left.

    3. Go 2 blocks to Brown Street.

D.  1. Go on Main Street to 3rd Street.

    2. Turn left.

    3. Go 1 block to Central Avenue.

E.  1. Go 2 blocks on Main Street to 2nd Street.

    2. Turn left.

    3. Go 2 blocks to Brown Street.

F.  1. Go 2 blocks on Main Street to 2nd Street.

    2. Turn left.

    3. Go 1 block to Central Avenue.

## Maps
### Part 2   *page 73*

Listen to the directions and use your finger to follow them on the map in your book. Start with your finger on the little person in the lower right corner of the map. At the end of each set of directions, you will come to a circle on the map. Write the correct letter in the circle.

PART 3                        Name _____

1st Street                              C

Oak Street | Brown Street | Central Avenue | Main Street

A  2nd Street

3rd Street          B          D

4th Street

**1**

**A.**  1. Go on Main Street to 2nd Street.
    2. Turn _____left_____.
    3. Go __3__ blocks to _____Oak Street_____.

**B.**  1. Go on Main Street to 3rd Street.
    2. Turn _____left_____.
    3. Go __2__ __blocks__ to Brown Street.

**C.**  1. Go on Main Street to _____1st_____ Street.
    2. Turn _____left_____.
    3. Go __1__ block to ____Central____ Avenue.

**D.**  1. Go __1__ block on _____Main_____ Street.
    2. Turn _____left_____.
    3. Go __1__ block to ____Central____ Avenue.

## Maps
**Part 3**  *page 74*
Listen to the directions and look at them in your book.
Write the missing words on the blanks in your book.  **1**

Now listen to the directions again. Use your finger
to follow them on the map in your book. Start at the
little person in the lower right corner of the map. At
the end of each set of directions, write the correct letter on the map.  **1**

PART 4                    Name _____

A   1st Street
Oak Street          Brown Street          Central Avenue          Main Street

2nd Street      D                    C

3rd Street       B

4th Street

A.  1.  Go 3 blocks on Main Street to 1st Street.
    2.  Turn left.
    3.  Go 3 blocks to Oak Street.

B.  1.  Go 1 block on Main Street to 3rd Street.
    2.  Turn left.
    3.  Go 2 blocks to Brown Street.

C.  1.  Go 2 blocks on Main Street to 2nd Street.
    2.  Turn left.
    3.  Go 1 block to Central Avenue.

D.  1.  Go 2 blocks on Main Street to 2nd Street.
    2.  Turn left.
    3.  Go 2 blocks to Brown Street.

## Maps
**Part 4**  *page 75*
Listen to the directions and write them on the lines in your book.  [1]

Now listen to the directions again. Use your finger to follow them on the map in your book. Start at the little person in the lower right corner of the map. At the end of each set of directions, write the correct letter on the map.  [1]

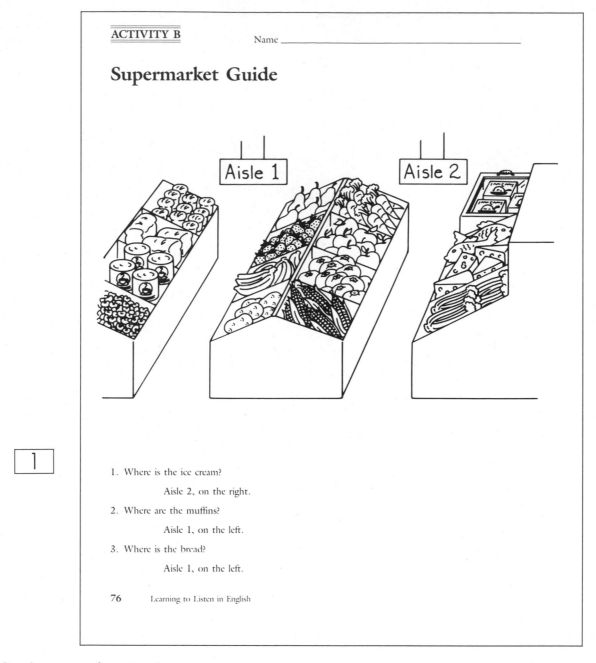

## Activity B: Supermarket Guide  *pages 76 and 77*

Listen to the questions and answers. Write the missing words on the blanks in your book. Look at the map if you need help. ☐ 1

Name _____

4. Where is the _____ coffee _____ ?

   Aisle __1__ , on the _____ left _____ .

5. Where is the _____ fish _____ ?

   Aisle __2__ , on the _____ right _____ .

6. Where is the _____ cheese _____ ?

   Aisle __2__ , on the _____ right _____ .

7. Where are the _____ pears _____ ?

   Aisle __1__ , on the _____ right _____ .

8. __Where are the strawberries?__

   Aisle __1__ , on the _____ right _____ .

9. __Where are the bananas?__

   Aisle __1__ , on the _____ right _____ .

10. __Where are the tomatoes?__

    __Aisle 2, on the left.__

11. __Where are the beans?__

    __Aisle 1, on the left.__

12. __Where is the celery?__

    __Aisle 2, on the right.__

13. __Where is the corn?__

    __Aisle 2, on the left.__

14. __Where are the carrots?__

    __Aisle 2, on the left.__

15. __Where are the apples?__

    __Aisle 2, on the left.__

16. __Where are the potatoes?__

    __Aisle 1, on the right.__

# Unit 8: Zoo Animals

## Activity A: Zoo Animals

**Part 1**  *page 78*
Listen to the names of these animals. Look at the words and pictures in your book. ☐1

PART 2                    Name _____

rhinoceros      hippopotamus      kangaroo      orangutan

flamingo      duck      zebra      turtle

goat      panda      moose      oryx

lion      seal      giraffe

Unit 8: Zoo Animals    79

1

**Zoo Animals**
**Part 2**  *page 79*
Listen and write the name of each animal by its picture.  1

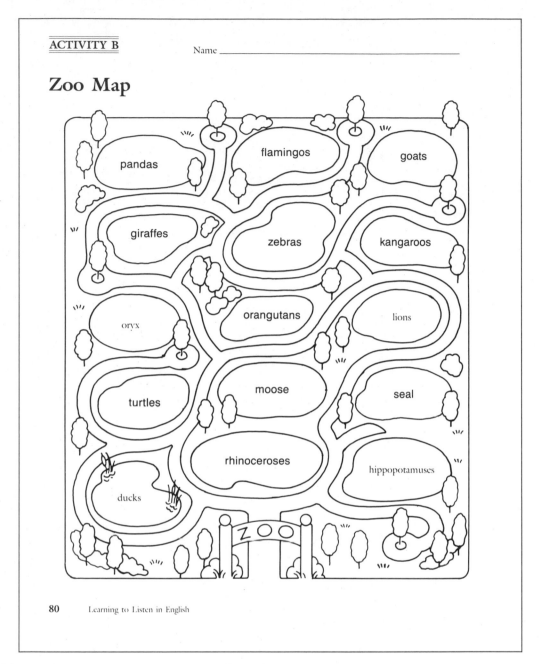

ACTIVITY B                    Name _____

# Zoo Map

pandas

flamingos

goats

giraffes

zebras

kangaroos

oryx

orangutans

lions

turtles

moose

seal

rhinoceroses

hippopotamuses

ducks

ZOO

## Activity B:  Zoo Map   *page 80*

Listen to the questions and answers. Write the names of the animals on the zoo map.

1. Where are the rhinoceroses?
   *Between the hippopotamuses and the ducks.*

2. Where are the goats?
   *In the upper right.*

3. Where are the kangaroos?
   *Between the goats and the lions.*

4. Where are the orangutans?
   *Between the oryx and the lions.*

5. Where are the flamingos?
   *Next to the goats.*

6. Where are the zebras?
   *Next to the kangaroos.*

7. Where are the turtles?
   *Between the oryx and the ducks.*

8. And the seal?
   *Between the lions and the hippopotamuses.*

9. How about the pandas?
   *In the upper left.*

10. And the moose?
    *Between the orangutans and the rhinoceroses.*

11. And where are the giraffes?
    *Next to the zebras.*

## ACTIVITY C

Name _____

# Map Directions

**PART 1**

1. north
2. northeast
3. east
4. southeast
5. south
6. southwest
7. west
8. northwest

1. __north__

8. __northwest__

2. __northeast__

7. __west__

3. __east__

6. __southwest__

4. __southeast__

5. __south__

**PART 2**

north

northwest

northeast

west

east

southwest

southeast

south

1

(Students will hear each direction only one time.)

## Activity C: Map Directions

**Part 1** *page 81*
Listen and write the directions on the lines in your book. 1

**Map Directions**
**Part 2** *page 81*
Listen again to the directions. This time they are not in order. Write them on the correct lines in your book.

south, east, north, west, northeast, southeast, northwest, southwest

ACTIVITY D          Name _____

# Another Zoo Map

**northwest**

ducks
flamingos
turtles
seals

**northeast**

rhinoceroses
zebras
goats
oryx

**southwest**

giraffes
hippopotamuses
lions

**southeast**

kangaroos
orangutans
pandas
moose

1

1. Where are the rhinoceroses?

    In the northeast section.

2. Where are the kangaroos?

    In the southeast section.

3. Where are the ducks?

    In the northwest section.

4. Where are the giraffes?

    In the southwest section.

5. Where are the hippopotamuses?

    __In the southwest section._____

## Activity D: Another Zoo Map   *pages 82 and 83*

Listen to the questions and answers. Write the missing answers in your book. ☐ 1

Now listen to these sentences. Write the name of each animal in the correct section in your book.

1. The rhinoceroses are in the northeast section.
2. The kangaroos are in the southeast section.
3. The ducks are in the northwest section.
4. The giraffes are in the southwest section.
5. The hippopotamuses are in the southwest section.
6. The orangutans are in the southeast section.
7. The flamingos are in the northwest section.
8. The zebras are in the northeast section.
9. The turtles are in the northwest section.
10. The goats are in the northeast section.
11. The pandas are in the southeast section.
12. The oryx are in the northeast section.
13. The moose are in the southeast section.
14. The lions are in the southwest section.
15. The seals are in the northwest section.

Name _____

6. Where are the orangutans?

    In the southeast section. _____

7. Where are the flamingos?

    In the northwest section. _____

8. Where are the zebras?

    In the northeast section. _____

9. Where are the turtles?

    In the northwest section. _____

10. Where are the goats?

    In the northeast section. _____

11. Where are the pandas?

    In the southeast section. _____

12. Where are the oryx?

    In the northeast section. _____

13. Where are the moose?

    In the southeast section. _____

14. Where are the lions?

    In the southwest section. _____

15. Where are the seals?

    In the northwest section. _____

**ACTIVITY E**             Name _____

# Bigger and Smaller

1

1. Which is bigger, a rhinoceros or a duck?

    A rhinoceros is bigger.

2. Which is smaller, a rhinoceros or a duck?

    A duck is smaller.

3. Which is bigger, a giraffe or a flamingo?

    A giraffe.

4. Which is smaller?

    A flamingo.

5. Which is bigger, a hippopotamus or a kangaroo?

    A hippopotamus is bigger.

6. Which is smaller?

    A kangaroo is smaller.

7. Which is bigger, a zebra or a turtle?

    A zebra.

8. Which is smaller?

    A turtle.

**Activity E:** *Bigger* and *Smaller*   *page 84*

Listen to the questions and answers. Look at the pictures in your book. Write the missing answers on the lines.   1

ACTIVITY F                  Name _____

# Zoo Animals and Their Origins

1. Where do hippopotamuses live?     In Africa.

2. Where do kangaroos live?          In Australia.

3. Where do pandas live?             In China.

4. Where do moose live?              In Russia.

5. Where do lions live?              In Africa.

6. Where do seals live?              In Canada.

7. Where do orangutans live?         In Borneo and Sumatra.

8. Where do zebras live?             In Africa.

9. Where do oryx live?               In Saudi Arabia.

## Activity F:  Zoo Animals and Their Origins  *page 85*

Listen to the questions and answers. Write the answers on the lines in your book. Look at the map if you need help.  ⬜1

## Unit 9: Names, Addresses, and Phone Numbers

# Names

1. What is your name?    Diana Phomin.    Spell it, please.
   D-I-A-N-A    P-H-O-M-I-N.

2. What is your name?    Edith Wernick.    How do you spell it?
   E-D-I-T-H    W-E-R-N-I-C-K.

3. First name?    Frances, F-R-A-N-C-E-S.
   Last name?    Berger, B-E-R-G-E-R.
   Middle initial?    L.

4. What is your name?    Wendy Steiner.    Spell it.
   W-E-N-D-Y    S-T-E-I-N-E-R.

5. What is your name?    Joe Brown.    Spell it.
   J-O-E    B-R-O-W-N.

6. First name?    Joe, J-O-E.    Last name?
   Brown, B-R-O-W-N.
   Middle initial?
   R.

# Unit 9: Names, Addresses, and Phone Numbers

## Activity A: Names  *page 86*

Listen to the questions and answers. Write the missing answers in your book.  1

1

### ACTIVITY B

Name _____

# Phone Numbers

1. What is your phone number?  555–2066.
2. What is your phone number?  Area code (602) 555–2066.
3. What is your phone number?  555–0911.
4. And the area code?  305.
5. What is your phone number?  _____ (201) 555–2565 _____.
6. What is your phone number?  _____ (219) 555–0244 _____.
7. What is your phone number?  _____ (303) 555–1622 _____.
8. What is your phone number?  _____ (406) 555–4433 _____.
9. What is your phone number?  _____ (806) 555–0521 _____.
10. What is your phone number?  _____ (612) 555–3760 _____.

### ACTIVITY C

# Area Codes

1. The area code for Montana is ___406___.
2. The area code for South Carolina is ___803___.
3. The area code for Arkansas is ___501___.
4. In Nevada, the area code is ___702___.
5. In Maine, the area code is ___207___.
6. The area codes for Massachusetts are ___413___ and ___617___.
7. The area codes for Florida are ___904___, ___305___, and ___813___.
8. The area codes for Virginia are ___703___ and ___804___.
9. In New Jersey, the area codes are ___201___ and ___609___.
10. In California, the area codes are ___707___, ___916___, ___415___, ___209___, ___408___, ___805___, ___213___, ___714___, ___818___, and ___619___.

Unit 9: Names, Addresses, and Phone Numbers    87

2

## Activity B:  Phone Numbers  *page 87*

Listen to the questions and answers. Write the missing phone numbers on the lines in your book.  1

## Activity C:  Area Codes  *page 87*

Listen to the sentences and write the area codes on the lines in your book. Look at the map if you need help.  2

Name _____

# Addresses

**Main Street**

1

1. What is your address?

    1588 Main Street.

2. What is your address?

    1600 Main Street, Apartment 105.

3. What is your address?

    1600 Main Street, Apartment __210__.

4. What is your address?

    1600 Main Street, Apartment __320__.

5. What is your address?

    __1600__ Main Street, Apartment __410__.

6. What is your address?

    __1628__ Main Street.

7. What is your address? __1632__ Main Street.

    What number?    1632.

8. What is your address?

    __1636__ Main Street.

9. What is your address?

    __1628A__ Main Street.

## Activity D: Addresses  *page 88*

Listen to the questions and answers. Write the missing numbers on the lines in your book. Look at the picture if you need help.    1

1

<u>ACTIVITY E</u>    Name _____

# Names, Addresses, and Phone Numbers

**PART 1**

1. Mary Bruder, M-A-R-Y  B-R-U-D-E-R
   1204 Main Street
   (304) 555–8945

2. Margaret Dwyer, M-A-R-G-A-R-E-T  D-W-Y-E-R
   300 Main Street
   (900) 555–7655

3. Marie Myer, M-A-R-I-E  M-Y-E-R
   2507 Central Avenue
   (301) 555–9681

4. Richard Feldman, R-I-C-H-A-R-D
   F-E-L-D-M-A-N
   2700 Central Avenue
   ( 213 ) 555 - 7786

5. David  Rand , D-A-V-I-D  R-A-N-D
   932 Main Street
   ( 608 ) 555 - 0031

6. Sue  Williams , S-U-E
   W-I-L-L-I-A-M-S
   1437 Central Avenue
   ( 418 ) 555 - 8741

7. Peter  Hanson , P-E-T-E-R
   H-A-N-S-O-N
   37201 Main Street
   ( 703 ) 555 - 5322

8. Sandra  Jones , S-A-N-D-R-A
   J-O-N-E-S
   200 E. Main Street
   ( 814 ) 555 - 6301

## Activity E: Names, Addresses, and Phone Numbers

**Part 1** *page 89*
Listen to the names, addresses, and phone numbers.
Write the missing information on the lines in your book.  1

Name _____

|      | Name | Address | Phone Number |
|------|------|---------|--------------|
| 1.   | yes  | no      | yes          |
| 2.   | yes  | yes     | yes          |
| 3.   | no   | yes     | no           |
| 4.   | yes  | yes     | yes          |
| 5.   | yes  | yes     | no           |
| 6.   | yes  | no      | yes          |
| 7.   | yes  | yes     | yes          |
| 8.   | yes  | no      | yes          |

## Names, Addresses, and Phone Numbers
**Part 2**  *page 90*
Listen to the information. When you hear a name, address, or phone number, write "yes" in the correct box. Write "no" in the box for anything you don't hear.

1. Amy Brown, 555–7391
2. Joe Smith, 200 E. Oak Street, 555–2004
3. 301 Central Avenue
4. Mary Brown, 16 Brown Road, 555–0056
5. Don Jones, 3442 Oak Street
6. Donna Smith, 555–9900
7. Carlos Vallejo, 266 Brown Road, 555–8334
8. Maggie Smith, 555–7732

ACTIVITY F

Name _____

# The Phone Book

**Brown** Linn 116 Central Ave . . . . . . . . . . . . .555–3409
**Brown** Loric 243 Brown Rd . . . . . . . . . . . . . .555–9672
**Brown** Louis F 6711 E. Central Ave . . . . . . .555–9034
**Brown** M 1103 Main St . . . . . . . . . . . . . . . . .555–9700
**Brown** M K 306 1st St . . . . . . . . . . . . . . . . .555–4500
**Brown** Matt and Ann 674 Main St . . . . . . . .555–0066
**Brown** Norman and Adrienne 600A Oak . . . .555–1156
**Brown** Pauline E 313 University . . . . . . . . . .555–1154

**Jones** Tracy R 215 Main St . . . . . . . . . . . . . .555–3004
**Jones** Trudy 3119 Central Ave . . . . . . . . . . .555–1928
**Jones** Virginia C 310 Oak St . . . . . . . . . . . .555–8884
**Jones** W W 3016 Central Ave . . . . . . . . . . . .555–8923
**Jones** Walter 2151 Main St . . . . . . . . . . . . .555–5774
**Jones** William D 200 E. Main St . . . . . . . . . .555–0905
**Jones** William F 1672 W. Main St . . . . . . . . .555–5612
**Jones** Willie V 5001 Central Ave . . . . . . . . . .555–6688

**Smith** Joan 211 Central Ave . . . . . . . . . . . . .555–5081
**Smith** John B 23 Main St . . . . . . . . . . . . . . .555–2284
**Smith** John F 247 Central Ave . . . . . . . . . . . .555–1006
**Smith** John J 964 2nd St . . . . . . . . . . . . . . .555–3386
**Smith** John L 3402 3rd St . . . . . . . . . . . . . .555–7774
**Smith** John Lee 2206 1st St . . . . . . . . . . . . .555–7676
**Smith** John T 230 E. Central Ave . . . . . . . . .555–9265
**Smith** Johnnie 1004 Main St . . . . . . . . . . . .555–5535

| Name | Address | Phone Number |
|---|---|---|
| 1. Linn Brown | 116 Central Avenue | 555–3409 |
| 2. Johnnie Smith | 1004 Main Street | 555–5535 |
| 3. W. W. Jones | 3016 Central Avenue | 555–8923 |
| 4. John F. Smith | 247 Central Avenue | 555–1006 |
| 5. M. K. Brown | 306 1st Street | 555–4500 |
| 6. Louis F. Brown | 6711 E. Central Avenue | 555–9034 |
| 7. Norman and Adrienne Brown | 600A Oak | 555–1156 |
| 8. John Lee Smith | 2206 1st Street | 555–7676 |
| 9. Willie V. Jones | 5001 Central Avenue | 555–6688 |
| 10. John T. Smith | 230 E. Central Avenue | 555–9265 |

Unit 9: Names, Addresses, and Phone Numbers    **91**

## Activity F: The Phone Book *page 91*

Listen to these names, addresses, and phone numbers. Write them in your book. 1

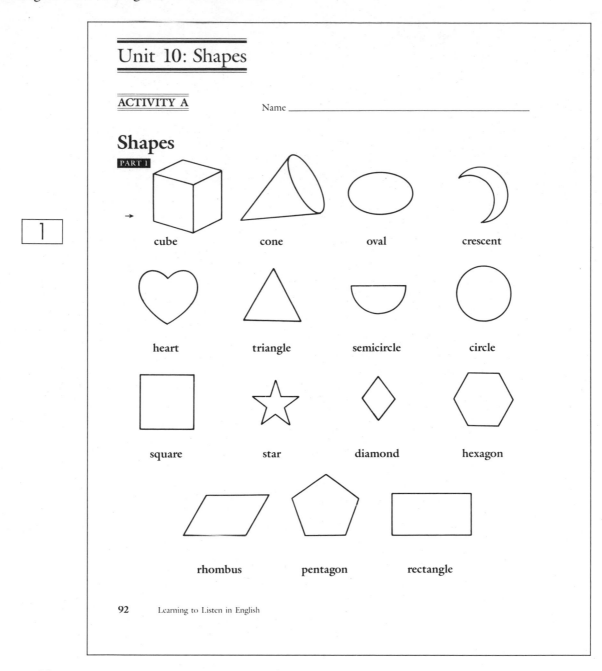

## Unit 10: Shapes

**ACTIVITY A:  Shapes**

**Part 1**  *page 92*
Listen to the names of these shapes. Look at the words
and pictures in your book.  | 1 |

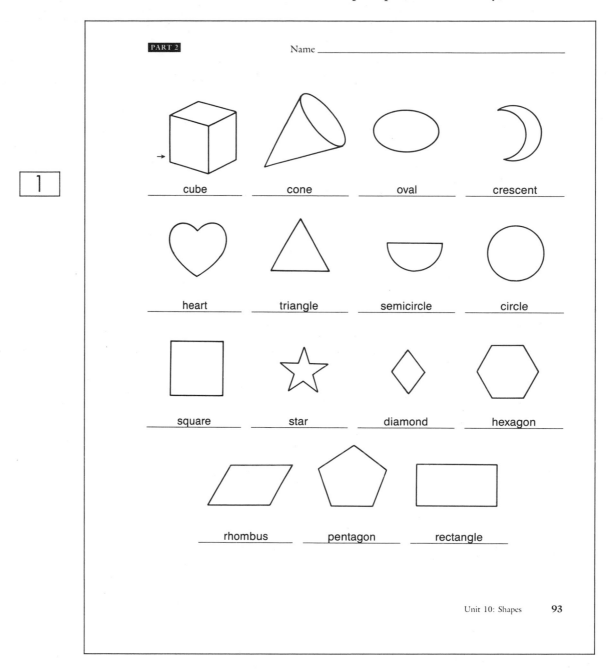

**Shapes**
**Part 2**   *page 93*
Listen and write the name of each shape by its picture.   1

<u>**ACTIVITY B**</u>     Name _____

# Sides
**PART 1**

1

1. How many sides does a cube have?
   ___6___.

2. What about a triangle?
   ___3___.

3. A square?
   ___4___.

4. How about a star?
   ___10___.

5. A diamond?
   ___4___.

6. And a hexagon?
   ___6___.

7. What about a rhombus?
   ___4___.

8. And a pentagon?
   ___5___.

9. And a rectangle, how many sides does a rectangle have?
   ___4___.

## Activity B: Sides

**Part 1**  *page 94*
Listen to the questions and answers. Write the answers in your book. Look at the pictures if you need help.  1

PART 2                    Name _____

| | 3 | 4 | 5 | 6 | 7 | 8 | 9 | 10 |
|---|---|---|---|---|---|---|---|---|
| 1. cube | | | | ✔ | | | | |
| 2. triangle | ✔ | | | | | | | |
| 3. square | | ✔ | | | | | | |
| 4. star | | | | | | | | ✔ |
| 5. diamond | | ✔ | | | | | | |
| 6. hexagon | | | | ✔ | | | | |
| 7. pentagon | | | ✔ | | | | | |
| 8. rectangle | | ✔ | | | | | | |
| 9. rhombus | | ✔ | | | | | | |

## Sides

**Part 2**  *page 95*

Listen to the sentences. Write the name of each shape on the line in your book. Then put an ✔ in the box under the number of sides the shape has.

1. A cube has six sides.
2. A triangle has three sides.
3. A square has four sides.
4. A star has ten sides.
5. A diamond has four sides.
6. A hexagon has six sides.
7. A pentagon has five sides.
8. A rectangle has four sides.
9. A rhombus has four sides.

ACTIVITY C                Name _____

# Upper and Lower

| upper left | upper right |
|---|---|
| lower left | lower right |

1

1. Draw a cube in the upper left.

2. Draw a cone in the upper right.

3. Draw a crescent in the lower left.

4. Draw a heart in the lower right.

5. Draw a triangle in the upper right.

6. Draw a semicircle in the upper left.

7. Draw a circle in the lower right.

8. Draw a _____square_____ in the lower right.

9. Draw a _____heart_____ in the lower left.

10. Draw a _____hexagon_____ in the lower left.

11. Draw a _____rhombus_____ in the upper right.

12. Draw a _____pentagon_____ in the upper left.

13. Draw a _____circle_____ in the lower left.

14. Draw a _____semicircle_____ in the lower right.

15. Draw an _____oval_____ in the upper right.

## Activity C: *Upper* and *Lower*   page 96

Listen and follow the directions. In sentences 9 through 15, you will also write the missing words in the blanks.

1

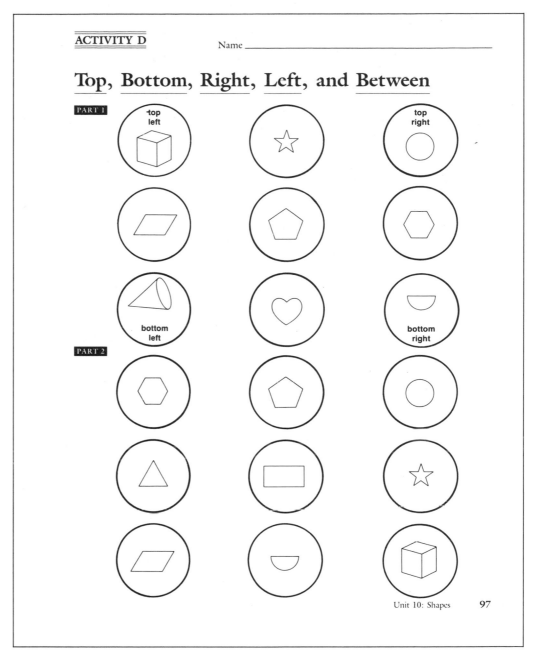

ACTIVITY D                    Name _____

# Top, Bottom, Right, Left, and Between

PART 1

PART 2

Unit 10: Shapes        97

## Activity D: *Top, Bottom, Right, Left,* and *Between*

**Part 1** *page 97*
Listen and follow the directions.

1. Draw a cube in the top left.
2. Draw a cone in the bottom left.
3. Draw a rhombus between the cube and the cone.
4. Draw a circle in the top right.
5. Draw a semicircle in the bottom right.
6. Draw a hexagon between the circle and the semicircle.
7. Draw a pentagon between the rhombus and the hexagon.
8. Draw a star between the cube and the circle.
9. Draw a heart between the cone and the semicircle.

*Top, Bottom, Right, Left,* and *Between*
**Part 2** *page 97*
Listen and follow the directions.

1. Draw a cube in the bottom right.
2. Draw a rhombus in the bottom left.
3. Draw a semicircle between the cube and the rhombus.
4. Draw a circle in the top right.
5. Draw a hexagon in the top left.
6. Draw a pentagon between the circle and the hexagon.
7. Draw a star between the cube and the circle.
8. Draw a triangle between the rhombus and the hexagon.
9. Draw a rectangle between the star and the triangle.

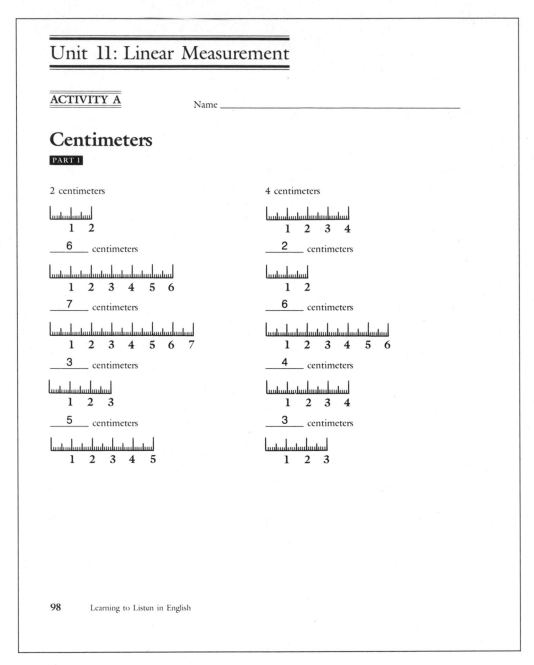

## Unit 11: Linear Measurement

### Activity A: Centimeters

**Part 1**  *page 98*
Listen and write the correct numbers in your book.

two centimeters, four centimeters

six centimeters, two centimeters

seven centimeters, six centimeters

three centimeters, four centimeters

five centimeters, three centimeters

1

PART 2   Name _____

1. The line is ___5___ centimeters long.

|ili|ili|ili|ili|ili|ili|ili|ili|ili|
1   2   3   4   5

2. The pencil is ___9___ centimeters long.

3. The paper clip is ___5___ centimeters long.

4. The ___key___ is ___5___ centimeters ___ long.

5. The ___knife___ is ___11___ centimeters ___ long.

6. The ___arrow___ is ___9___ centimeters ___ long.

7. The ___finger___ is ___6___ centimeters ___ long.

Unit 11: Linear Measurement    99

**Centimeters**
**Part 2**  *page 99*
Listen to the sentences. Write the missing numbers and
words in your book.    1

Name _____

1

1. How long is the line?

   It is ___5___ centimeters long.

2. How long is the pencil?

   It is ___9___ centimeters long.

3. How long is the paper clip?

   ___5___ centimeters long.

4. How long is the _____key_____?

   ___5___ centimeters.

5. How long is the _____knife_____?

   ___11___ centimeters.

6. How long is the _____arrow_____?

   ___9___ _____centimeters_____.

7. How long is the _____finger_____?

   ___6___ _____centimeters_____.

**Centimeters**
**Part 3**  *page 100*
Listen to the questions and answers. Write the missing numbers and words in your book. 1

1

### ACTIVITY B

Name _____

## Inches

**PART 1**

1. The key is ___2___ inches long.

2. The knife is ___4___ inches long.

3. The brush is ___5___ inches long.

4. The ____line____ is ___3___ inches long.

5. The ____arrow____ is ___4___ ____inches____ long.

6. The ____pencil____ is ___6___ ____inches____ long.

7. The ____finger____ is ___2___ ____inches____ long.

## Activity B: Inches

**Part 1** *page 101*

Listen to the sentences. Write the missing numbers and words in your book.

1

PART 2                          Name _____

1

1. How long is the key?

    It is ___2___ inches long.

2. What about the brush? How long is it?

    ___5___ inches long.

3. How many inches long is the _____knife_____?

    ___4___.

4. How long is the _____line_____?

    ___3___ inches.

5. How many inches long is the _____arrow_____?

    ___4___.

6. How long is the _____finger_____?

    ___2___ _____inches_____.

7. How many inches long is the _____pencil_____?

    ___6___.

**Inches**
**Part 2**  *page 102*
Listen to the questions and answers. Write the missing numbers and words in your book.   1

<u>ACTIVITY C</u>                    Name _____

# Greater than, Less than, and Equal to

**PART 1**

1    *(Students will hear each sentence; they will not hear the sentence in its shortened form.)*

1. A 4-centimeter line is longer than a 2-centimeter line.

   ___4 cm.___    ___>___    ___2 cm.___

2. A 3-centimeter line is shorter than a 6-centimeter line.

   ___3 cm.___    ___<___    ___6 cm.___

3. A 5-centimeter line is equal to a 5-centimeter line.

   ___5 cm.___    ___=___    ___5 cm.___

4. An 8-centimeter pencil is longer than a 5-centimeter pencil.

   ___8 cm.___    ___>___    ___5 cm.___

5. A 3-centimeter arrow is shorter than a 7-centimeter arrow.

   ___3 cm.___    ___<___    ___7 cm.___

6. A 10-centimeter line is equal to a 10-centimeter line.

   ___10 cm.___    ___=___    ___10 cm.___

7. A 7-centimeter line is equal to a 7-centimeter line.

   ___7 cm.___    ___=___    ___7 cm.___

8. A 12-centimeter pen is shorter than an 18-centimeter pen.

   ___12 cm.___    ___<___    ___18 cm.___

Unit 11: Linear Measurement    **103**

## Activity C: Greater than, Less than, and Equal to

**Part 1** *page 103*
Listen to the sentences and read them in your book.
Then write each sentence in a shortened form.    1

PART 2                              Name _____

**1**

(Students will hear each sentence; they will not hear the sentence in its shortened form.)

1. A 3-inch line is longer than a 2-inch line.

   __3 in.__   __>__   __2 in.__

2. A 1-inch line is shorter than a 5-inch line.

   __1 in.__   __<__   __5 in.__

3. A 3-inch line is the same length as a 3-inch line.

   __3 in.__   __=__   __3 in.__

4. A 5-inch knife is longer than a 4-inch knife.

   __5 in.__   __>__   __4 in.__

5. A 7-inch brush is shorter than a 9-inch brush.

   __7 in.__   __<__   __9 in.__

6. A 10-inch pencil is the same length as a 10-inch pencil.

   __10 in.__   __=__   __10 in.__

7. A 3-inch key is shorter than a 4-inch key.

   __3 in.__   __<__   __4 in.__

8. An 8-inch line is the same length as an 8-inch arrow.

   __8 in.__   __=__   __8 in.__

**Greater than, Less than, and Equal to**
**Part 2** *page 104*
Listen to the sentences and read them in your book.
Then write each sentence in a shortened form.   **1**

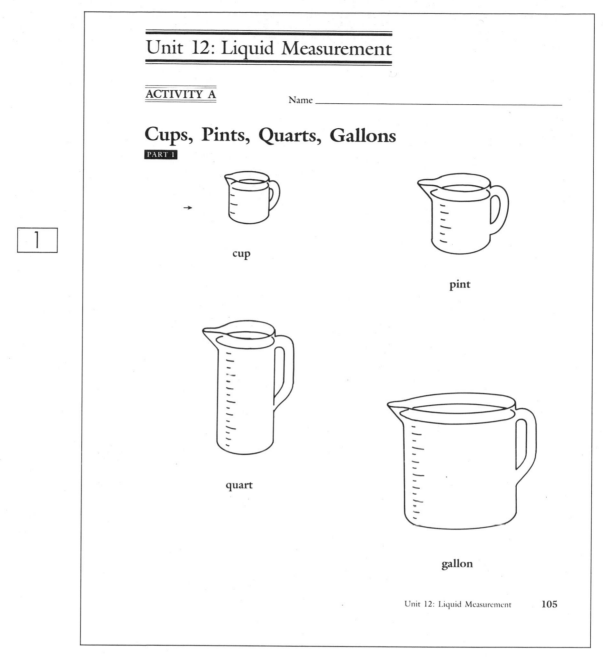

# Unit 12: Liquid Measurement

<u>ACTIVITY A</u>          Name _____

## Cups, Pints, Quarts, Gallons
PART 1

→ cup

pint

quart

gallon

1

# Unit 12:  Liquid Measurement

## Activity A:  Cups, Pints, Quarts, Gallons

**Part 1**  *page 105*
Listen to the names of these units of measurement.
Look at the words and pictures in your book. ⬜ 1

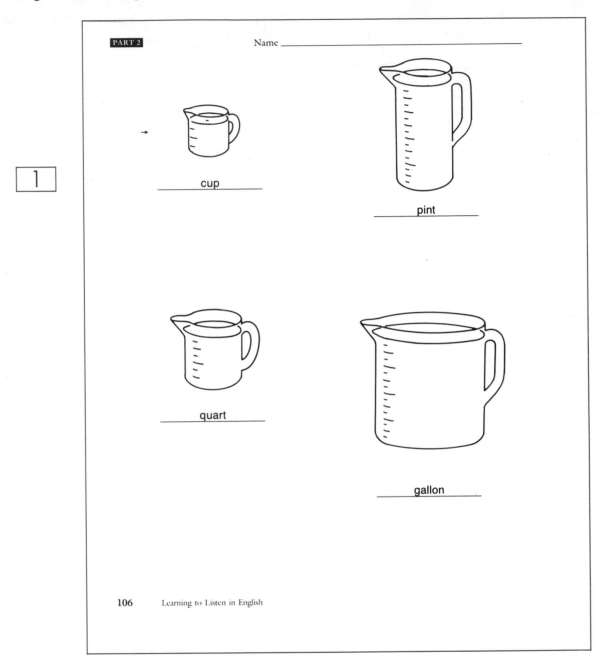

**Cups, Pints, Quarts, Gallons**
**Part 2**  *page 106*
Listen and write the name of each unit of measurement by its picture.   1

PART 3

Name _____

1

a cup of coffee
**1 cup**

a bottle of milk
**1 gallon**

a mug of coffee
**1 pint**

a cup of soup
**1 cup**

a carton of milk
**1 quart**

a can of soup
**1 pint**

Unit 12: Liquid Measurement    **107**

## Cups, Pints, Quarts, Gallons
**Part 3**  *page 107*
Listen to the names of these foods and their amounts.
Look at the pictures in your book.  1

<u>ACTIVITY B</u>                    Name _____

# How Many?

1

1. How many cups in a pint?

   There are 2 cups in a pint.

2. How many cups in a quart?

   4 cups.

3. How many cups in a gallon?

   32.

4. How many pints in a quart?

   2.

5. How many pints in a gallon?

   8.

6. How many quarts in a gallon?

   4.

7. How many cups in a _____ pint _____?

   ___ 2 ___.

8. How many cups in a _____ quart _____?

   ___ 4 ___.

9. How many _____ cups _____ in a _____ gallon _____?

   ___ 32 ___.

10. How many _____ pints _____ in a _____ quart _____?

    ___ 2 ___.

11. ___ How many pints in a gallon? _____

    ___ 8 ___.

12. ___ How many quarts in a gallon? _____

    ___ 4 ___.

108    Learning to Listen in English

## Activity B: How Many? *page 108*

Listen to the questions and answers. Write the miss-
ing words and numbers in your book.  | 1 |

ACTIVITY C                    Name _____

# Which Is More?

PART 1

1. Which is more, a gallon or a cup?

   A gallon is more.

2. Which is more, a quart or a pint?

   A quart.

3. Which is more, 2 quarts or 1 quart?

   2 quarts.

4. Which is more, 2 pints or a gallon?

   A gallon.

1

2

PART 2

1. Which is more, a gallon or a quart?

   __A gallon._____

2. Which is more, a quart or a pint?

   __A quart._____

3. Which is more, a cup or _____a pint_____?

   __A pint._____

Unit 12: Liquid Measurement    **109**

## Activity C:  Which Is More?

**Part 1**  *page 109*
Listen to the questions and answers and read them
in your book.  [1]

## Which Is More?

**Part 2**  *pages 109 and 110*
Listen to the questions and answers. Write them in
your book.  [2]

Name _____

4. Which is more, 2 pints or _____ 3 pints _____?

    __ 3 pints. _____

5. Which is more, _____ a cup or a gallon _____?

    __ A gallon. _____

6. __ Which is more, 2 cups or 4 cups? _____

    __ 4 cups. _____

7. __ Which is more, 3 cups or a pint? _____

    __ A pint. _____

8. __ Which is more, 2 quarts or a gallon? _____

    __ A gallon. _____

9. __ Which is more, 2 pints or 3 cups? _____

    __ 2 pints. _____

10. __ Which is more, 2 gallons or 10 quarts? _____

    __ 10 quarts. _____

11. __ Which is more, 4 pints or 3 quarts? _____

    __ 3 quarts. _____

ACTIVITY D                Name _____

# Full or Empty?

**full**    **empty**

1

1. Is the pint empty or full?

   _____ It is empty. _____

2. Is the pint empty or full?

   _____ Full. _____

3. Is the glass empty or full?

   _____ Empty. _____

4. Is the glass empty or full?

   _____ Full. _____

5. Is the coffee mug empty or full?

   _____ Full. _____

6. Is the coffee mug empty or full?

   _____ Empty. _____

Unit 12: Liquid Measurement    **111**

## Activity D:  Full or Empty?  *page 111*

Listen to the questions and answers. Write the answers on the lines in your book. Look at the pictures if you need help.    1

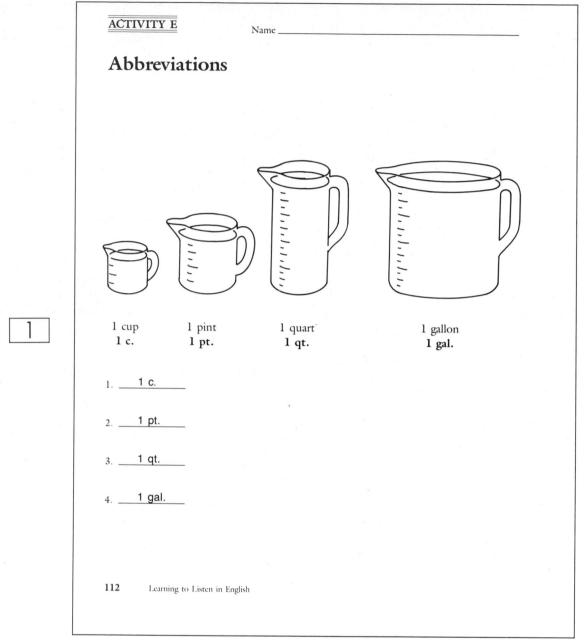

## Activity E:  Abbreviations  *page 112*

Listen to the names of these units of measurement.
Look at the pictures, words, and abbreviations in your
book.  1

Now listen and write the abbreviations on the lines
in your book.  1

# Unit 13: The Body

### ACTIVITY A

Name _____

## The Body

**PART 1**

1

eyes    nose    mouth    face

shoulders    elbow    fingers    arms

legs    back    neck    ear

foot    toes    hand    knee

# Unit 13: The Body

## Activity A: The Body

**Part 1**  *page 113*
Listen to the parts of the body. Look at the words and pictures in your book.    1

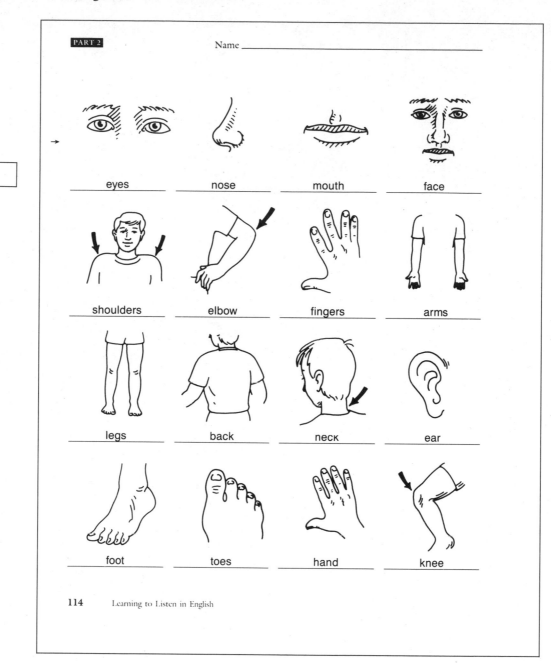

**The Body**
**Part 2**  *page 114*
Listen and write the name of each body part by its
picture.  `1`

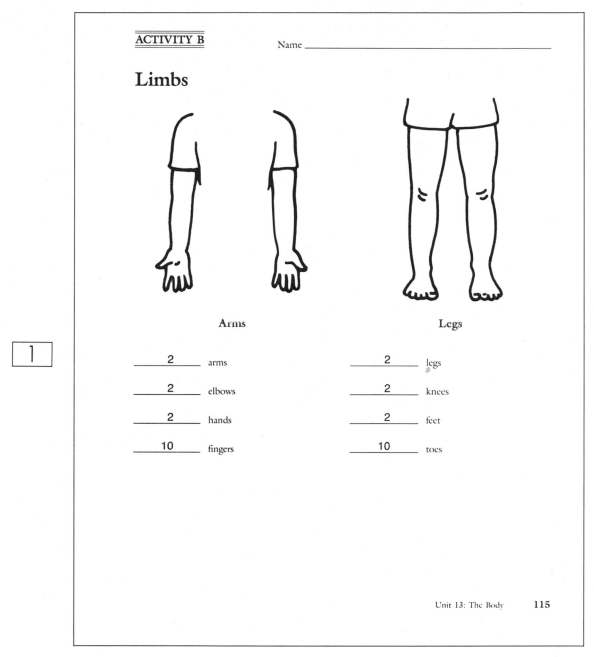

ACTIVITY B                    Name _____

# Limbs

Arms                                    Legs

| 1 |

_____2_____ arms              _____2_____ legs

_____2_____ elbows            _____2_____ knees

_____2_____ hands             _____2_____ feet

_____10_____ fingers          _____10_____ toes

Unit 13: The Body    **115**

## Activity B: Limbs  *page 115*

Listen and write the correct numbers on the lines in
your book.  | 1 |

ACTIVITY C

Name _____

# Upper or Lower?

1

| | Upper | Lower |
|---|---|---|
| arms | ✓ | |
| back | ✓ | |
| ears | ✓ | |
| elbows | ✓ | |
| eyes | ✓ | |
| face | ✓ | |
| fingers | ✓ | |
| feet | | ✓ |
| hands | ✓ | |
| knees | | ✓ |
| legs | | ✓ |
| mouth | ✓ | |
| neck | ✓ | |
| nose | ✓ | |
| shoulders | ✓ | |
| toes | | ✓ |

## Activity C:  Upper or Lower?  *page 116*

Listen to the parts of the body and look at the picture
in your book. Decide whether each body part is in
the upper or lower half of the body. Put a check mark
in the correct column next to each body part.  1

1

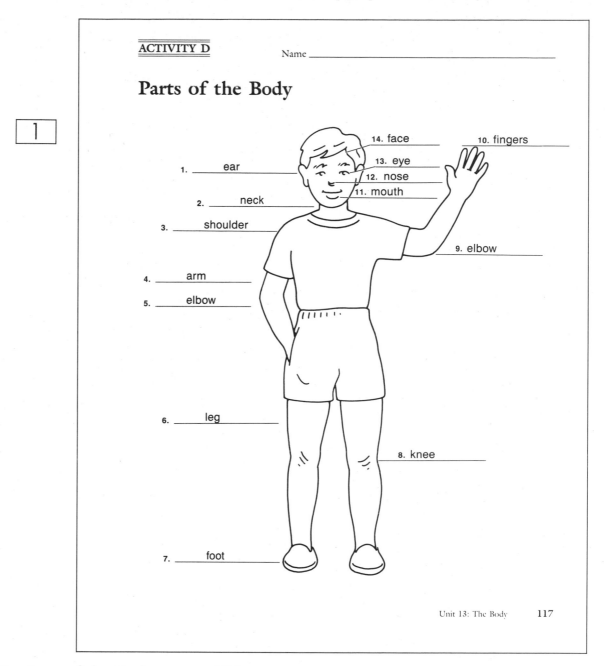

Name _____

## Parts of the Body

14. face     10. fingers

1. _____ ear     13. eye

12. nose

11. mouth

2. _____ neck

3. _____ shoulder

9. elbow

4. _____ arm

5. _____ elbow

6. _____ leg

8. knee

7. _____ foot

## Activity D:  Parts of the Body   *page 117*

Listen to the parts of the body. Write them on the correct lines in your book.   1

ACTIVITY E

Name _____

**Actions**

PART 1

jumping        sleeping        exercising

swimming       walking         running

reading        leaning         crawling

118      Learning to Listen in English

## Activity E:  Actions

**Part 1**  *page 118*

Listen to the names of these actions. Look at the words
and pictures in your book.  ⬜1

PART 2                    Name _____

1

| | | |
|---|---|---|
| jumping | sleeping | exercising |
| swimming | walking | running |
| reading | leaning | crawling |

Unit 13: The Body     119

**Actions**
**Part 2**  *page 119*
Listen and write the name of each action by its picture.    1

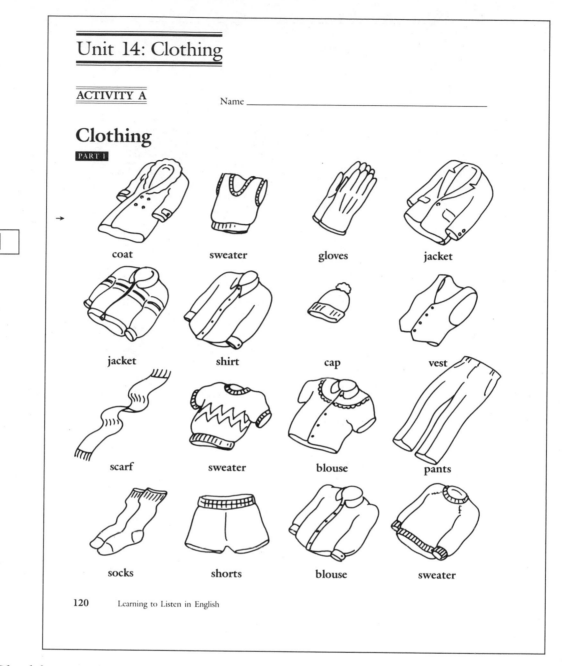

# Unit 14: Clothing

## ACTIVITY A

Name _____

# Clothing

**PART 1**

→

| | | | |
|---|---|---|---|
| coat | sweater | gloves | jacket |
| jacket | shirt | cap | vest |
| scarf | sweater | blouse | pants |
| socks | shorts | blouse | sweater |

120    Learning to Listen in English

# Unit 14: Clothing

## Activity A: Clothing

**Part 1**  *page 120*

Listen to the names of these types of clothing. Look
at the words and pictures in your book.  ☐1

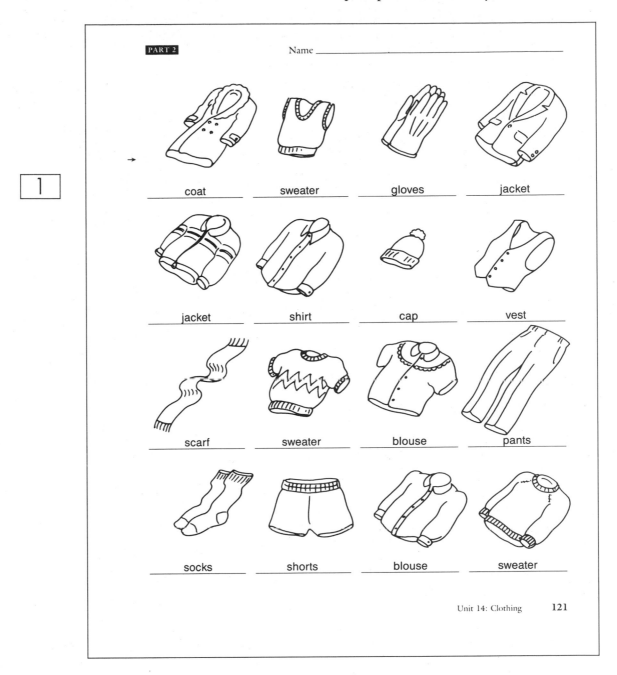

**Clothing**
**Part 2** *page 121*
Listen and write the name of each type of clothing by its picture. ⬚1

**ACTIVITY B**          Name _____

# Cold Weather or Hot Weather?
**PART 1**

**Cold Weather**

_____ coat _____

_____ jacket _____

_____ scarf _____

_____ shirt _____

_____ blouse _____

_____ vest _____

_____ sweater _____

_____ pants _____

_____ gloves _____

_____ cap _____

**Hot Weather**

_____ shorts _____

_____ pants _____

_____ blouse _____

_____ sweater _____

_____ socks _____

## Activity B: Cold Weather or Hot Weather?

**Part 1**  *page 122*

Listen to the dialogue. Write the names of the clothing in the correct columns for cold weather and hot weather.

What do you wear in cold weather?

In cold weather? A coat or a jacket, a scarf, a shirt or a blouse, a vest and a sweater, pants, gloves, and a cap.

What do you wear in hot weather?

Shorts or pants, a blouse or a sweater, and socks.

PART 2                    Name _____

|  | Cold Weather | Hot Weather |
|---|---|---|
| coat | ✔ | |
| scarf | ✔ | |
| sweater | ✔ | |
| sweater | | ✔ |
| gloves | ✔ | |
| cap | ✔ | |
| blouse | | ✔ |
| blouse | ✔ | |
| jacket | ✔ | |
| socks | ✔ | ✔ |
| shirt | ✔ | ✔ |
| shorts | | ✔ |
| coat | ✔ | |
| vest | ✔ | |
| pants | ✔ | ✔ |
| sweater | ✔ | ✔ |

Unit 14: Clothing    123

## Cold Weather or Hot Weather?
**Part 2**  *page 123*

Listen to the dialogue. Put check marks in the correct columns next to each type of clothing to show whether it is worn in cold weather or in hot weather.

Do you wear a coat in cold weather or in hot weather?

In cold weather! How about a scarf?

Cold weather! A sweater?

Long sleeves, in cold weather; sleeveless, in hot weather. And gloves?

Cold weather! What about a cap?

Cold weather, again! A blouse?

Short sleeves, in hot weather; long sleeves, in cold weather. A jacket?

Cold weather. Socks?

Cold weather and hot weather! A shirt?

Cold weather and hot weather, too! Shorts?

In hot weather. What about a coat?

Cold weather. A vest?

Cold weather. Pants?

Cold weather and hot weather. A sweater with short sleeves?

Cold weather and hot weather!

ACTIVITY C          Name _____

# Long Sleeves, Short Sleeves, or Sleeveless?
PART 1

long sleeves

short sleeves

sleeveless

1

## Activity C: Long Sleeves, Short Sleeves, or Sleeveless?

**Part 1**  *page 124*
Listen and look at the words and pictures in your book.

PART 2            Name _____

|  | long sleeves | short sleeves | sleeveless |
|---|---|---|---|
| coat | ✔ | | |
| jacket | ✔ | | |
| jacket | ✔ | | |
| sweater | ✔ | | |
| sweater | | ✔ | |
| shirt | | ✔ | |
| shirt | | ✔ | |
| vest | | | ✔ |
| sweater | | | ✔ |
| blouse | ✔ | | |

## Long Sleeves, Short Sleeves, or Sleeveless?
**Part 2**  *page 125*

Listen to the dialogue. For each piece of clothing, put a check mark in the box under *long sleeves, short sleeves,* or *sleeveless.*

My coat has long sleeves.

So does my jacket.

I have a jacket with long sleeves, too.

How about your sweater?

It has long sleeves.

Mine has short sleeves. So does my shirt.

My shirt has short sleeves, and my vest is sleeveless.

My sweater is sleeveless, but my blouse has long sleeves.

ACTIVITY D

ACTIVITY D                     Name _____

# Shopping for Clothes
**PART 1**

| | | |
|---|---|---|
| 1. blouse, short sleeves | $22.99 | |
| 2. pants | $28.00 | |
| 3. shirt, long sleeves | $21.95 | |
| 4. scarf | $12.00 | |
| 5. gloves | $10.00 | |
| 6. sweater, long sleeves | $30.00 | |
| 7. sweater, short sleeves | $26.00 | |
| 8. sweater, sleeveless | $24.00 | |
| 9. socks | $3.75 | |
| 10. vest | $23.00 | |
| 11. shorts | $9.99 | |
| 12. caps | $8.50 | |
| 13. jackets | $45.00 | |
| 14. coat | $75.00 | |

## Activity D: Shopping for Clothes

**Part 1** *page 126*
Listen to the dialogue. Write the price of each item in your book.

What does a blouse with short sleeves cost?

$22.99. What do pants cost?

$28.00. How about a shirt with long sleeves?

$21.95. What about a scarf?

$12.00. Gloves are $10.00. I need a sweater. How much is a sweater with long sleeves?

$30.00. What about a short-sleeved sweater?

$26.00. And a sleeveless sweater costs $24.00. Do you know how much socks cost?

$3.75. What will I have to pay for a vest?

$23.00. How about shorts? What do shorts cost?

$9.99. And caps are $8.50. Do you know what jackets cost?

$45.00, and a good coat is $75.00.

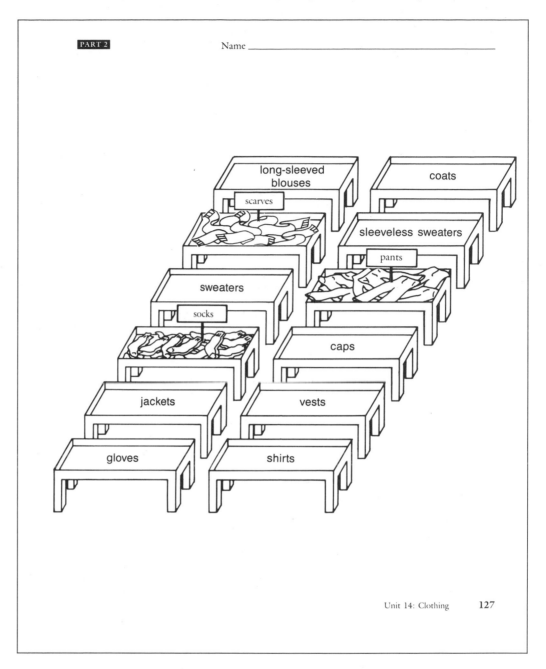

PART 2          Name _____

long-sleeved blouses        coats

scarves

sleeveless sweaters

pants

sweaters

socks

caps

jackets        vests

gloves        shirts

Unit 14: Clothing    127

## Shopping for Clothes
**Part 2**  *page 127*
Listen to the questions and answers. Write the names of the clothes on the store map.

Where are the coats?

At the back of the store, on the right.

And the gloves?

At the front of the store, on the left.

Sleeveless sweaters?

Between the coats and the pants.

Jackets?

On the left, between the gloves and the socks.

What about the shirts? Where are the shirts?

On the right, at the front of the store.

And the vests?

Next to the jackets.

And where can I find the caps?

Between the pants and the vests.

What about the sweaters? Where are the sweaters?

Between the scarves and the socks.

Do you have any blouses with long sleeves?

Yes, of course. At the back of the store, on the left.

*emballage*
*empaquetage*

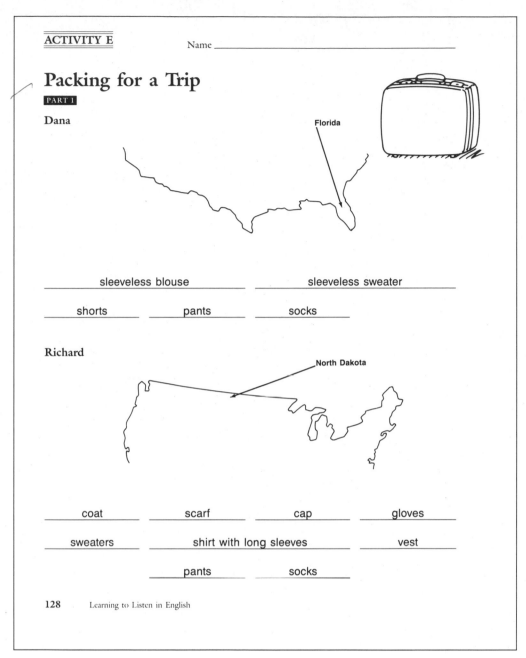

ACTIVITY E                          Name _____

# Packing for a Trip
**PART 1**
**Dana**

Florida

_____ sleeveless blouse _____    _____ sleeveless sweater _____

_____ shorts _____  _____ pants _____  _____ socks _____

**Richard**

North Dakota

_____ coat _____  _____ scarf _____  _____ cap _____  _____ gloves _____

_____ sweaters _____  _____ shirt with long sleeves _____  _____ vest _____

_____ pants _____  _____ socks _____

128    Learning to Listen in English

## Activity E: Packing for a Trip

**Part 1** *page 128*

Listen to the dialogues. Write the names of the clothing each person is packing on the lines in your book.

Hi, Yasuko!

Hi, Dana, what are you doing?

I'm packing for a trip to Florida.

When are you leaving?

July 15. Let me see, I've got a sleeveless blouse, a sleeveless sweater, shorts, pants, and socks.

Have a good trip!

Hey, Steve, how have you been?

Hi, Richard. You are packing?

Yes. I am going to North Dakota on February 12.

Don't forget your coat, scarf, cap, gloves, and sweaters. You had better take a shirt with long sleeves, a vest, pants, and socks, too.

Thanks, I will.

PART 2                        Name _____

**Dana:** I'm going on a trip to Florida.

**Yasuko:** When are you leaving?

**Dana:** July 1.

**Yasuko:** What are you taking?

_____ sleeveless blouse _____    _____ sleeveless sweater _____

_____ shorts _____    _____ pants _____    _____ socks _____

**Richard:** I'm going on a trip to North Dakota.

**Steve:** When are you leaving?

**Richard:** February 12.

**Steve:** What are you taking?

_____ coat _____    _____ scarf _____    _____ cap _____    _____ gloves _____

_____ sweaters _____    _____ shirt with long sleeves _____    _____ vest _____

_____ pants _____    _____ socks _____

Unit 14: Clothing    **129**

**Packing for a Trip**
**Part 2**  *page 129*
Listen to the dialogues. Write the names of the clothing each person is taking on the lines in your book.

I'm going on a trip to Florida.

When are you leaving?

July 1.

What are you taking?

A sleeveless blouse, a sleeveless sweater, shorts, pants, and socks.

I'm going on a trip to North Dakota.

When are you leaving?

February 12.

What are you taking?

My coat, a scarf, a cap, gloves, sweaters, a shirt with long sleeves, a vest, pants, and socks.

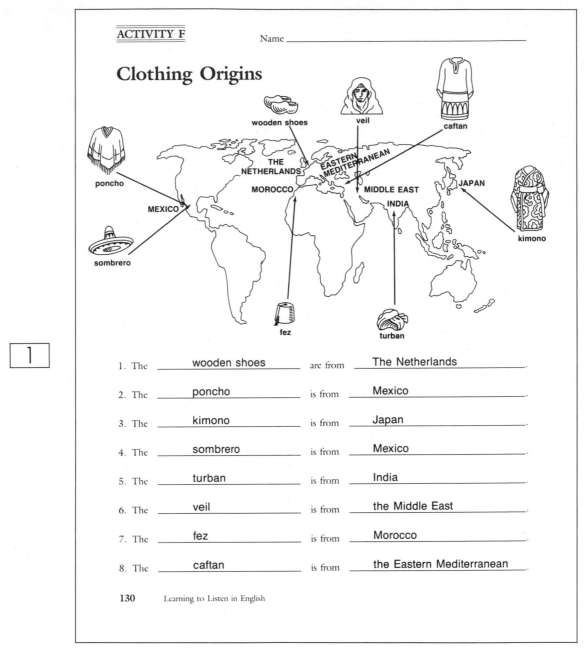

ACTIVITY F    Name _____

# Clothing Origins

1. The _____ wooden shoes _____ are from _____ The Netherlands _____.

2. The _____ poncho _____ is from _____ Mexico _____.

3. The _____ kimono _____ is from _____ Japan _____.

4. The _____ sombrero _____ is from _____ Mexico _____.

5. The _____ turban _____ is from _____ India _____.

6. The _____ veil _____ is from _____ the Middle East _____.

7. The _____ fez _____ is from _____ Morocco _____.

8. The _____ caftan _____ is from _____ the Eastern Mediterranean _____.

**130**    Learning to Listen in English

## Activity F: Clothing Origins  *page 130*

Listen to the sentences. Write the names of the clothing and the countries on the lines in your book. Look at the map if you need help.  1

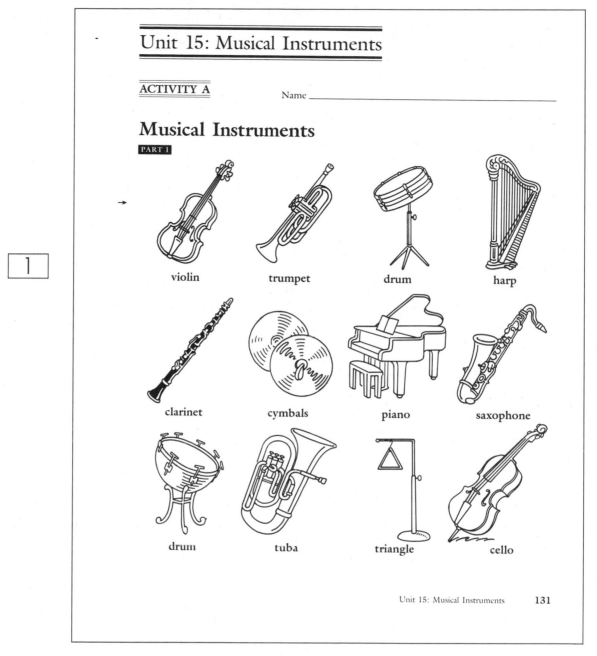

## Unit 15: Musical Instruments

ACTIVITY A

Name _____

### Musical Instruments

PART 1

violin    trumpet    drum    harp

clarinet    cymbals    piano    saxophone

drum    tuba    triangle    cello

Unit 15: Musical Instruments    131

## Unit 15:  Musical Instruments

### Activity A:  Musical Instruments

**Part 1**  *page 131*

Listen to the names of these musical instruments. Look
at the words and pictures in your book.  [1]

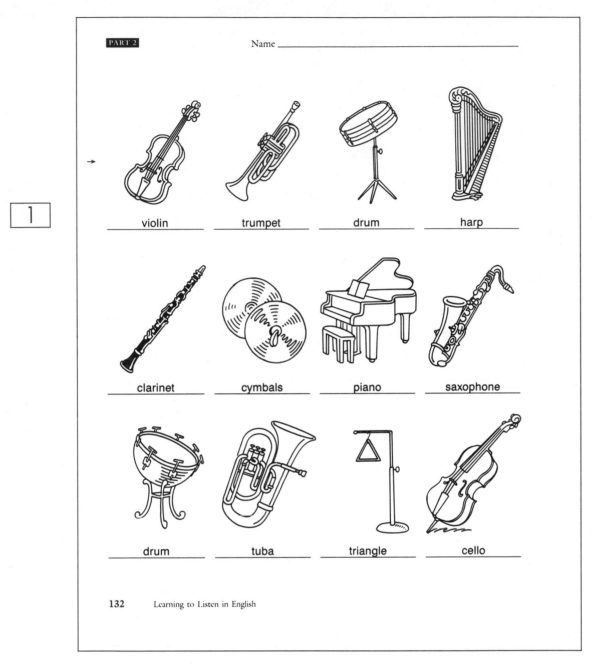

PART 2    Name _____

| | | | |
|---|---|---|---|
| violin | trumpet | drum | harp |
| clarinet | cymbals | piano | saxophone |
| drum | tuba | triangle | cello |

1

**Musical Instruments**
**Part 2**  *page 132*
Listen and write the name of each musical instrument
by its picture.  1

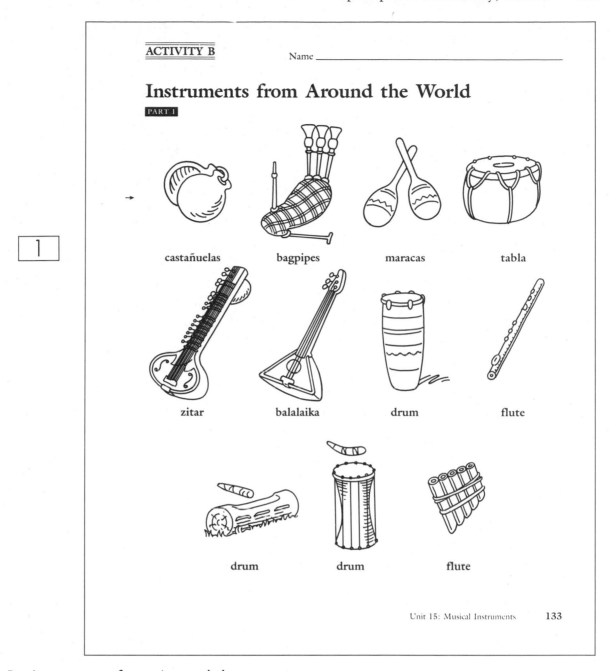

ACTIVITY B

Name _____

# Instruments from Around the World
PART 1

1

| | | | |
|---|---|---|---|
| castañuelas | bagpipes | maracas | tabla |
| zitar | balalaika | drum | flute |
| drum | drum | flute | |

## Activity B: Instruments from Around the World

**Part 1**  *page 133*
Listen to the names of these instruments. Look at the words and pictures in your book. 1

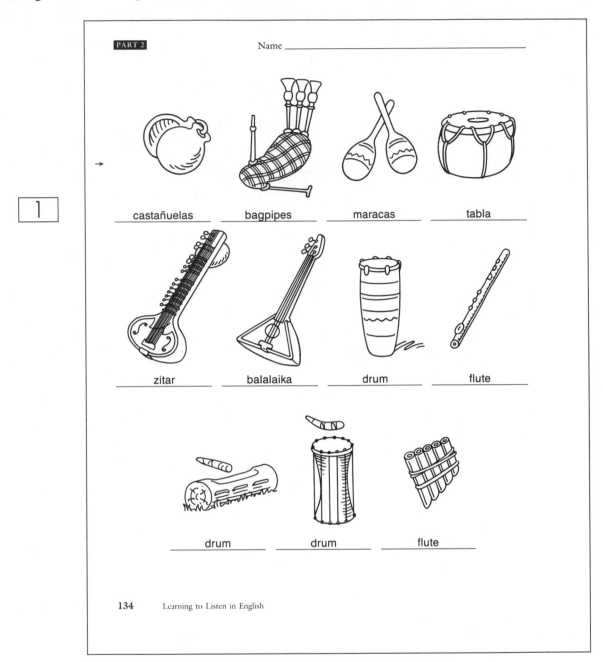

**Instruments from Around the World**
**Part 2** *page 134*
Listen and write the name of each instrument by its
picture. 1

ACTIVITY C          Name _____

# Sections of the Orchestra

PART 1

| Wind | Percussion | Brass | String |
|------|-----------|-------|--------|
| clarinet | triangle | tuba | violin |
| saxophone | cymbals | trumpet | cello |
|  | piano |  |  |
|  | drum |  |  |
|  | maracas |  |  |

Unit 15: Musical Instruments    135

## Activity C:  Sections of the Orchestra

**Part 1**  *page 135*

Listen to the questions and answers. Write the names of the instruments in the correct columns.

What are the wind instruments?

The clarinet and the saxophone.

What instruments are in the percussion section?

The triangle, cymbals, piano, drum, and maracas.

How about the brass section?

The tuba and the trumpet.

What about string instruments? Can you name two?

The violin and the cello.

|  | Wind | Percussion | Brass | String |
|---|---|---|---|---|
| violin |  |  |  | ✔ |
| trumpet |  |  | ✔ |  |
| drums |  | ✔ |  |  |
| harp |  |  |  | ✔ |
| tuba |  |  | ✔ |  |
| saxophone | ✔ |  |  |  |
| clarinet | ✔ |  |  |  |
| cello |  |  |  | ✔ |
| cymbals |  | ✔ |  |  |
| piano |  | ✔ |  |  |
| triangle |  | ✔ |  |  |
| maracas |  | ✔ |  |  |

**Sections of the Orchestra**
**Part 2**  *page 136*

Listen to the dialogue. Put a check mark in the correct column next to the name of each instrument.

Is the violin a string instrument?

Yes, and the trumpet is brass.

How about the drums?

Percussion. But the harp is a string.

Where does the tuba go?

It is a brass instrument.

Which are the wind instruments?

The saxophone and the clarinet. Can you name another string instrument?

Yes, the cello. How about the cymbals?

They are percussion. So are the piano and the triangle.

And the maracas?

They are also percussion.

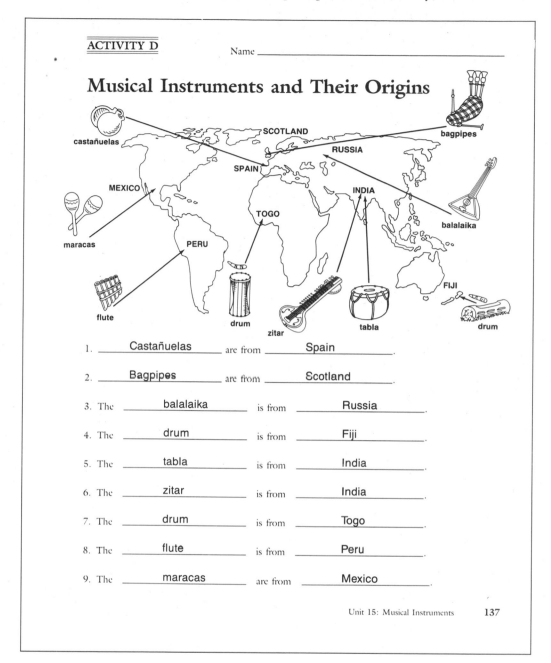

ACTIVITY D

Name _____

# Musical Instruments and Their Origins

castañuelas
SCOTLAND
bagpipes
RUSSIA
SPAIN
MEXICO
INDIA
TOGO
balalaika
maracas
PERU
FIJI
flute
drum
zitar
tabla
drum

1. _____Castañuelas_____ are from _____Spain_____.

2. _____Bagpipes_____ are from _____Scotland_____.

3. The _____balalaika_____ is from _____Russia_____.

4. The _____drum_____ is from _____Fiji_____.

5. The _____tabla_____ is from _____India_____.

6. The _____zitar_____ is from _____India_____.

7. The _____drum_____ is from _____Togo_____.

8. The _____flute_____ is from _____Peru_____.

9. The _____maracas_____ are from _____Mexico_____.

Unit 15: Musical Instruments    137

## Activity D: Musical Instruments and Their Origins  *page 137*

Listen to the sentences. Write the names of the instruments and the countries on the lines in your book. Look at the map if you need help.

1. Castañuelas are from Spain.
2. I know, and bagpipes are from Scotland.
3. Russia is the home of the balalaika.
4. And Fiji is where the Fijian drum comes from.
5. The tabla is from India.
6. So is the zitar.
7. The African drum is from Togo.
8. And the South American flute, from Peru.
9. The maracas are from Mexico.

# NTC ESL/EFL TEXTS AND MATERIAL
## Junior High—Adult Education

**Computer Software**
Amigo
Basic Vocabulary Builder on Computer

**Language and Culture Readers**
Beginner's English Reader
Cultural Encounters in the U.S.A.
Passport to America series
 California Discovery
 Adventures in the Southwest
 The Coast-to-Coast Mystery
 The New York Connection
Discover America series
 (text/audiocassettes)
 California
 Chicago
 Florida
 Hawaii
 New England
 New York
 Texas
 Washington, D.C.
Looking at American Signs
Looking at American Food
Looking at American Recreation
Looking at American Holidays
Time: We the People (text/audiocassettes)

**Text/Audiocassette Learning Packages**
Speak Up! Sing Out! 1, 2
Listen and Say It Right in English!

**Transparencies**
Everyday Situations in English

**Duplicating Masters and Blackline Masters**
Easy Vocabulary Games
Vocabulary Games
Advanced Vocabulary Games
Play and Practice!
Basic Vocabulary Builder
Practical Vocabulary Builder
Beginning Activities for English
 Language Learners
Intermediate Activities for English
 Language Learners
Advanced Activities for English
 Language Learners

**Language-Skills Texts**
English with a Smile 1, 2
English Survival Series
 Building Vocabulary A, B, C
 Recognizing Details A, B, C
 Identifying Main Ideas A, B, C
 Writing Sentences and Paragraphs
  A, B, C
 Using the Context A, B, C
English Across the Curriculum 1, 2, 3
Essentials of Reading and Writing
 English 1, 2, 3
Everyday English 1, 2, 3, 4
Learning to Listen in English
 (workbook/audiocassettes)
Listening to Communicate in English
 (workbook/audiocassettes)

Communication Skillbooks 1, 2, 3
Living in the U.S.A. 1, 2, 3
Basic Everyday Spelling Workbook
 (audiocassettes)
Practical Everyday Spelling Workbook
 (audiocassettes)
Advanced Readings and Conversations
Practical English Writing Skills
Express Yourself in Written English
Campus English
Speak English!
Read English!
Write English!
Orientation in American English
Building English Sentences
Grammar for Use
Grammar Step-by-Step
Listening by Doing
Reading by Doing
Speaking by Doing
Vocabulary by Doing
Writing by Doing
Look, Think and Write

**Survival-Skills Texts**
Building Real Life English Skills
Everyday Consumer English
Book of Forms
Essential Life Skills series
Finding a Job in the United States
English for Adult Living 1, 2
Living in English
Prevocational English

**TOEFL Preparation**
NTC's Preparation Course for the
 TOEFL® (with 3 audiocassettes)
NTC's Practice Tests for the TOEFL®
 (with 3 audiocassettes)

**Dictionaries and References**
ABC's of Languages and Linguistics
Everyday American English Dictionary
Building Dictionary Skills in
 English (workbook)
Beginner's Dictionary of American
 English Usage
Beginner's English Dictionary
 Workbook
NTC's American Idioms Dictionary
NTC's Dictionary of American Slang
 and Colloquial Expressions
Essential American Idioms
Contemporary American Slang
Forbidden American English
101 American English Idioms
Idiom Workbook
Essentials of English Grammar
The Complete ESL/EFL Resource Book
Safari Grammar
Safari Punctuation
303 Dumb Spelling Mistakes
TESOL Professional Anthologies
 Grammar and Composition
 Listening, Speaking, and Reading
 Culture

For further information or a current catalog, write:
National Textbook Company
a division of *NTC Publishing Group*
4255 West Touhy Avenue
Lincolnwood, Illinois 60646-1975 U.S.A.